THIS IS A SPILL, THIS IS A SPELL

ULTRAMAGICA

NEW YORK

Words by C. M. Escabi
Book Cover by C. M. Escabi
Edits by Marion Bright
Author Portraits by Ryan Rodriguez

Excerpt from *The Alchemist* by Paulo Coelho

ISBN: 979-8-9879037-0-4

Published by Ultramagica, LLC
New York, NY
ultramagica.com

Printed in the United States of America

To my inner child

"Ruin is the road to
Transformation."

—Elizabeth Gilbert
Eat Pray Love

CONTENTS

IN THE MIDDLE

IN THE MIDDLE—*An Introduction*

It is only fitting to start this book in the middle.

Eleven years ago, I thought I would surely die over a boy who broke my heart. Little did I know that my heart was broken long before and it only took a little push from this boy to finally fall—it had been a long time coming after all. It was as though my lungs had collapsed and I could not breathe. I lapsed into a depressive episode that lasted many years, but after making the choice to live more fully, I muscled the strength to re-open my heart. At the pit of my stomach, I felt an immense desire to live and to experience a love so fulfilling that it would perpetually quench my parched soul. In the Valley of Dry Bones, life was breathed back into me in the form of hope.

Every so often throughout the past eleven years, I would flip the pages of my journals to remind myself of the girl I was—and to this day, I find that the words I scribbled during sadness were the instructions for my salvation. For without those words, I am uncertain whether I would have survived at all.

I always say, it is a beautiful thing to "feel deeply"—and as children and as teenagers, that is all we do. To feel every feeling and ride through the waves of emotions for the first time, for better and for worse, carries with it its own set of magic. We collect many firsts like an accomplishment in a video game or reading a book without pictures for the first time— and so it was for me like having a whole collection of firsts brought on by the fluctuations of hormones, the desire to be touched, and the yearning to be free. I wanted to burst out of my own skin yet was afraid that the world would persecute me if I did. So instead, I chose to lose myself in my internal dialogue of thoughts and words, and in the way my pen glided over paper in the dark.

I have lived more a life in my journals than I did in being, but those written words were real—as real as the untempered feelings of a child losing their best friend. I spent all that time during my adolescence years screaming. I screamed louder as the pages flipped and filled with ink, but no one heard. Not that I was looking and not that it would have mattered if they did, but my world was shrinking into metaphor, and reaching for the real fruits of life became figment. It wasn't until reading through the journals as an adult today that I finally came to understand that my screams could have only reached the one person who would have known how to put out my fires. I was looking for myself, a woman now in her Saturn Return, to reach within the pages and pull out little ol' me from drowning. No other person would have known how to maneuver the ocean of my pages to find me, and it is my hope that in reading these words, you will reach out for yourselves too. Extend a hand for every version of you that felt neglected, confused, unloved, and most often hurt by your own hands—or inner monologue. It is okay to not know how to begin to listen or lift yourself up, but I promise that you will, in time.

These pages are not another testimony of a Taurean girl gone mad over love. Rather, they are a testament to my inner child whose only wish was to be loved and love back. These pages are time capsules intended to explore the cracks of my psyche as I experienced them. This book is a long-winded apology letter to my womanhood. It comprises written spells for healing who I once was, saying goodbye to the ghosts of my pasts, and finding balance in newer ways of love.

This book is a compilation of sixty-three journal entries across six chapters written as a teenager with interjections and new musings as an older—though still young—adult. It is hard to say for sure which version(s) of myself came through which piece—and thus you will find that the subject throughout the book changes quite frequently. For each piece, you will find an astrological symbol referencing one of the zodiac signs in the below chart in its title. Each piece was either written to/with a particular person in mind who I loved or now love, or they were written for me (♉) as I processed trauma and surrendered into love when it presented itself. Although there is no specific order to which you should read these essays, the chapters represent an arc starting from my past and transcending into my present. You will find that certain astrological signs repeat across chapters being just as relevant now as they used to be then. There are also clues for each symbol connecting them to their pairing individual throughout the book.

These pages are the bone broth to my soul and if you find bits of yourself in them, I wish them to be for yours as well.

Please remember, this isn't the beginning and for sure as hell is not the ending, but the middle—for we are bound to meet here again when healing.

C. M. Escabi

ASTROLOGICAL SYMBOLS

♉ Taurus

♌ Leo

♏ Scorpio

♑ Capricorn

DESCENT ♏

I fell in love with a Scorpio. He had blue eyes like the ocean—a shark that thrashed havoc in my waters. He caught me three times, and each time I almost drowned. The last time, I barely made it out alive; but I never wanted anything else so badly. He brought out the good in me and oftentimes, the worst. I've never felt more loved nor more lonely at the same time, and yet I wanted to consume him entirely in my flames and to claim him as forever mine.

With him, I became the lover I swore I'd never be. I thought of myself as soft, self-less, and hid behind my laughs, but my knuckles soon calloused from rage and my body suited up in armor as I demanded more. My sweet demeanor became bitter. My edges turned sharp and jagged. It had seemed the monster in me collided with the monster in him.

Whoever I was becoming in his presence I did not recognize when reflected in his gleamy and watery skin, and it scared me. My insides churned as I came to terms with the onset on my transformation from Eve to Lilith. I metamorphosized from fragile and shy to assertive, resolute, and unswerving—and such power coursed through my veins relentlessly. When he saw my resiliency even within his grasp, the shark quit chasing, seeking another victim who would be submissive to his bite as easily as I had been before.

I was left to face myself, then. I mourned my past and made a grave out of tears for her. In distress, it was I who had caused my drowning this time. Grief acted as bricks tied to my feet and to the ocean floor where the sun's rays wouldn't dare reach, I descended to ruminate.

While the Scorpio continued his hunt, I died many times until I chose rebirth. Rather than staying trapped in my despair, I chose to break free from it— severing the cord that tied me to the ocean bottom. I swam up to shore where breath finally greeted me like an old friend.

My journey from caterpillar to butterfly, was challenging, and even now I'm sure I would find myself making difficult decisions and unfolding inevitably so again; for chaos loves chaos—even misery and all her company.

Despite the increased strength I've adopted in my descent, I stayed more water than fire. Stayed soft rather than rough. More accepting of the force that rides with me and I now embrace its fury with love.

Now I no longer fear such sharks of the likes of him when the only threat swimming in the water is a woman empowered.

AN INCANTATION ♉

If we were not too careful, we may find ourselves trapped in a demise of our own making. It is both a blessing and a curse. A liberator and an oppressor. Wars were started over it and countries gifted in its name. Even if it leaves, it regenerates when called and births laughter into a galaxy of stars. It is bold and audacious, yet soft like April rain bringing forth flowers from the winter's dead. Yes, it can bring back the dead. Reincarnate even the most damned of souls and breathe new life into the living too.

Some say that time is a testament to prove that it is true, while other say distance—and if we ever needed confirmation of its power, all we had to do was look toward the sky to witness how the celestial bodies have interacted for billions of years. They were born before us and will no doubt outlive us. The most beautiful affair we have all come to know is when the sun rises and sets with the moon not too far behind, engaging in a dance—forever apart, but always close by, and kept bound together in such beautiful chemistry when invoking an eclipse.

For centuries, their story left poets and storytellers searching for magic just as great within the microcosms of the flesh, and frequently encountering its shadow, hate, instead, with "I love you," being the most powerful spell.

BEFORE

OBLIVION ♏

You would think after all I've written about you
I'd remember more.
The fact is I don't. I don't even remember:

what it is you look like
or the way you smell
or the way you would make that smirk—
you know the one that would
get you out of trouble.

Now that I think about it,
I can't even remember your voice and
how you used to say my name like a whisper,
or how long it would take you to get ready
when everyone else would blame me
for our tardiness to dinner.

You used to have a way about you.
The way you carried yourself.
The way you thought you were always right.
The way you liked it when I said "mi amor."
The way you would sing in Italian at night.

To be honest, I really hated those Adidas sweats
and that annoying laugh you had that
sounded like the Joker—
If captions were a thing, yours would read:

"HA! HA! HA! HA!"

Most of all, I can't remember what changed.
Maybe you got tired of arguing
or being pushed away,
or maybe you had your own selfish reasons.

Maybe it was all three, and yet you're here again
wanting me to remember all of you
as if you never left in the first place.

But do you want to know what
I don't need help remembering?

I don't need help remembering
Being discarded and broken,
because that I could never forget.

SPLIT ♏

I have grown cold to protect
these fragile walls.
At this point nothing will phase me.

What are feelings?
What are tears?
What is pain?

You grow upset because it seems
that I do not care,
yet you mustn't forget:

You created this icy demeanor.

WHICH ONE IS IT? ♉

If it isn't love,
it is fear.

If it isn't fear,
it is love.

Sometimes,
it is both—
one just barely
surpassing
the other.

HOLD BACK ♏

I can show you all of me,
but it would take some time.

At first you must unravel me,
pull out the secrets stuffed and divined
like a ball of yarn.
As you make your way to my core,
I'd manifest myself in sentiments,
then mere words.
Itsy bitsy pieces are all you'd get.

It'd take you time and patience
to sleuth the riddle and
put me back together again
after the damage you'd sown.

At least this time, I am safe.
At least this time, I can give in to you enough
and hold back a little for myself.

This way you won't have the chance
to destroy all in one shot.
This way I could walk away
with only a scratch in soft flesh.

DECEMBER, DON'T BREAK MY HEART ♏

We are back where we ended: a couple of weeks before Christmas. A whole year has gone by, and I have lost and regained you all within the same time. December never fails to go and come again and so when the bare trees wither under its snow, I wonder too if I will be left out in the cold so barren and hungry.

On TV are the classic holiday flicks and the house smells of mulled wine and fir. Though this winter, I find my evenings are spent wrapped in wool blankets, my skin never fails to fill with goosebumps. I awake in a sense of foreboding that any day now Santa will retrieve you from under the tree.

When homes are gearing up for the season of giving and couples walking through Brooklyn Bridge Park come together and embrace the warmth of their bodies, I grown mistrustful of December. July and August have always had their way with us. They provided fuel for our fire and kept our flames strong, while sweet eats in October and November such as candies and pumpkin pies kept us full yet wanting more.

Now the city prepares to go into deep slumber, and I fear that your heart will sleep too; and like Goddess

Persephone, I would be lost in the underworld forever. I ask that this winter hold us together even when its fingers are already frigid. Even when holding on becomes painful. Even if holding on is all that is left for us to do to not get swept up in December's heartless blizzard.

And in case this is it, and December fails to deliver you again, may my heart strengthen to withstand the cold without you. May it hold me over till Spring—till May's flowers bloom and I can breathe again anew. May this season be the last time that I hesitate at the close of November.

May I look forward to meeting December, someday, once again.

MATCHES ♏

Your eyes used to gleam red
whenever you lit matches.

It ignited something inside you—
the way the match sparked with fire.

All day long, you would strike
a match and stare and the
fire danced before your eyes.

You would get lost in
fireworks and cigarette lighters.

I always wondered why you were
captivated by the dancing flames
almost to the point of obsession.

The fire within you ignited
passion as much as destruction

and the signs had always
been there.

THE STAR ♏

"Please don't go," were the last words he said to me in person.

I was fast walking to catch the bus with tears running down my face and my heart dragging on the floor a few paces behind. It was hard to see in front of me. December's fog came early and though it was cold, my heart felt colder. The concoction of the winter wind and my tears blurred my vision, and I was left to use my intuition to guide my way back home. The east river watched on as I rushed alongside it from the dorm room to the bus. The water remained still and quiet, as if knowing long before which way we were headed.

The walk from his dorm room to the bus stop was long enough for me to rethink and overthink. I tried to make sense of how the events prior unfolded.

"I don't think this is going to work anymore," he said over the phone the night before.

"I don't think I want *you* anymore..." He emphasized, and the conversation went quiet. Words could not escape my mouth. How could they? My throat closed in on me and I began to hyperventilate. Air escaped me as fast as my words leaving me breathless. In the middle of collecting myself and silence, he hung up. I dialed back but his phone went straight to voicemail, and soon enough I spent the whole night crying into my pillow and choking on my saliva—hoping that my wails would not wake my parents who slept in the room a door down from mines.

With what little energy I had in the morning, I chose to chase romance and skipped school. I hopped on a two-hour ride north first thing in the morning to reclaim our relationship. It is amazing how living in the same city could still put us hours away from each other.

This cannot be it, I thought. *I just must see him in person, and he'll understand...* But my life is not a movie, and our script never had a happy ending.

"I don't want to be with you anymore," he said again as I stood in the middle of his dorm room holding on to whatever dignity I had left.

"Okay," I managed to let out in the middle of an agonized sigh, and I ran.

"Crystal!" I heard faintly in the background, snapping me back into reality. I stopped and turned around. I saw him running towards me, and though I should have felt relieved, I felt anger. *How can he play with me like that? How much more damage is he willing to inflict?* I thought, and I quickly turned back around and rushed towards the bus.

In the distance before me, I saw what might have been a dream awake all along. Far in the distance a group in black swarmed. They swayed one way and then the other in what looked like swift calculated movements. Their feet shuffled in a dance, and they moved towards my direction.

He shouted my name once more, ringing louder, meaning he was closer behind.

"Leave me alone!" I screamed out.

The black mass grew near enough to finally see what, or rather who, they were. On their feet were roller blades. Their black habits flapped in the wind—a hard nudge stopped me in my tracks. He stood in front of me and doubled over trying to catch his breath. Holding up his hand, he exhaled "Please... don't... go..."

All my pain had accumulated into rage by this point, and I stepped up to his face and looked him dead in the eyes. Through gritted teeth I said, "You. Hurt. Me." The group skated past us in a flurry while we two stood still in the middle. On a cold December day, it seems that nuns in roller blades can be found skating throughout the Throggs Neck Peninsula.

His mouth closed and his face fell, as if a knee jerk

reaction. He remained still. I picked up my feet and walked past him, leaving him behind.

I feared to look back in case I would be turned into a pillar of salt.

I reached the bus stop shortly after and sat down on the bench. I contemplated the last two years of my life. I contemplated the years before it when we were also together, and of all the time we spent thinking of one another when we were young. They said we were too young to feel what we felt, but we felt it nonetheless, and we continued for the next six years to seek out each other. All that time now felt like a waste. My face felt numb, and my cheeks were frozen from the cold. I felt mentally and physically exhausted that I stopped crying, stopped thinking, and stared off into space.

In my peripheral vision, I saw movement. I looked up and saw a nun skate towards my direction in the distance. I stared on numbly. They skated closer until they were right before me. I looked up perplexed. I thought I had imagined their black and white habit flapping in the wind moments before, but here one was, less than a foot away.

With a sympathetic face, she reached into her pocket and pulled out a card. She motioned for me to take it. My right hand took the card and I looked at it. In the middle was a familiar face with brown hair past the shoulders.

"Jesus loves you," the nun said, clasping her hands.
"You are beautiful, and I will pray for you." She
bowed her head to me and then turned and skated
away. I looked down in my hands to gaze upon what
she bestowed upon me: a prayer card with a picture
of the Nazareth King, Jesus.

I chuckled out loud. *Of course you would make
yourself known at this moment, Jesus.* I smirked.
The last time I had prayed to God, I was in
elementary school, and since then, Jesus had taken
the back seat. Though I no longer resonated with
Him, I was touched by the spirit of this nun who had
the gall to reach out during my moment of crisis. She
had just witnessed the collapse of the Tower as I
struggled to escape the rubble for air. From my point
of view, all I could see was chaos and devastation.
From hers, she saw hope and opportunity.

I squeezed the prayer card in my hand. Despite how
fresh my wounds were, the nuns offered a beacon of
light. *Everything was going to be okay.*

My longing to get up and run back to him was
immense but I remained seated. The uncertainty of
being alone scared me, but I also had a renewed
sense of faith. The Universe—heck even God maybe—
had found their way to tell me that they haven't
forsaken me the same way I had them, and that this

painful ending was the start of something new. The end was nowhere near.

All I had to do was look up if I ever needed a reminder as to where I am headed. No matter the terrain, the stars will guide my way.

The bus eventually made its way to me. Its doors opened and I stood there at the precipice. "Once I get on, there will be no turning back," I whispered under my breath. The driver looked at me, puzzled, as I contemplated my next move. I breathed in deeply and mounted the bus; sitting down on the first seat I saw. The driver closed the bus doors and drove on slowly.

I looked out the window towards the East River and said goodbye to this part of the city for good.

THE ENDING

BROKEN HEARTED IN NEW YORK CITY ♉

New York City can either be easy or be tough on you. On most occasions, it is the latter. The winters here are harsh and with every year that goes by, the city feels colder than the last. Layers upon layers are necessary to keep warm and prevent your fingers from frostbite. I wonder if the frigid temperatures are the city's way of warning us; "prepare," it whispers: "build up layers so you are not exposed—so that you don't get hurt."

This city has its way of making you a cynic. You either have seen it all or seen nothing. If you nestle here long enough and have found some sort of comfort sandwiched between two strangers on the ACE or F train, you will find that nothing surprises here. How could it? The city is not accepting nor tolerant. It just is and it has created the perfect breeding ground for the loud, the weirdos, the eccentrics, and the loners to run wild. It is the concrete jungle after all.

If you ever find yourself strung over family drama or lost love, the city reminds you that there is more to worry about: the cold, the rise in rent, the cost of living, the dirt, the grime, the crime...

And sometimes, if you find yourself downtrodden, the city will open itself up to you too.

New York City stretches on in the matter of five boroughs—connecting enclaves of strangers and cultures through tunnels and bridges. For the folks living here, this city is the world. If anyone asks, the sun revolves around us, and if you are in the middle of Canal Street trying to make your way between the sea of tourists buying fake Prada and Louis Vuitton, bags and stuffing their faces with "street meat" from the halal carts, you are at the center of anything and everything—where all could happen.

There is much to see and neighborhoods to explore as far as Coney Island to the Bronx Zoo. There are numerous things that can divert your attention, including the constant flow of traffic and the flashing street lights to the music blasting from the neighbor's stereo on their balcony to the "showtime" boys soliciting tips during your commute home on the subway. It is rare to have an extended period without something pulling your focus away. You are never by yourself. Somehow, someone would make their way to you whether you invited them or not. The city flows with such intense electricity, magnetizing all.

But if you were not careful, this city could make you feel as lonely as it does alive. To the best that they can, its residents mind their own business. Look on and keep walking could be our motto had "Excelsior" not taken over. Struggle was not unusual, and the truth of the matter is, everyone has their own fair share of worries than the woes of others. If a hand was what you sought, you could stay waiting a long time. "Just try and keep it together" is the unspoken, shared goal.

New York City is the best and worst place to be when carrying a broken heart. It offers you an oasis to escape with adventure lurking at every corner. The number of things to do is endless and will have you at first distracted, and then healed, in time. But it also offers you a prison. Those same diverting corners could suck you into dreary alleys to wallow in and lose your sense of direction. It makes you a bed to lay in yet does not bother to tuck you in—leaving the decrepit fire escapes, cigarette smoke, and the moon to adorn your night sky. Rats come and go hoping to find a meal, but instead find you. In only a matter of time you could lose yourself entirely here.

This is what the city can do if you play the cards right, versus if the cards play you.

PEACE OF MIND ♉

Laying in this bathtub has become a new kind of ritual.

Here, I would come to unwind after a long day of doing and would take solace in the act of then doing nothing. I would sit here for hours dreaming, reminiscing of the six-year-old me who did the exact same thing many years ago. She'd dream of the people she'd meet; make up conversation as she made hats and beards out of bath suds in the tub. I wonder if she would've known that instead of imagining more, she would one day be craving simplicity and forgetting to find joy in bubble baths like this.

That one day she would instead be wishing for less heartache.

This bathtub was once my playground and now it has become my nursing bed bearing witness to a steady decline. It does not know which of its water it produced fresh and in bounty or was brought in by the tears of my own making, an ocean I have unintentionally conjured.

I lie here and the amount of time spent is as long as I did when I was younger. Hours would pass staring at the same white walls and marble tiles before me except now there is an accumulation of grime around the faucet, and the grout between the tiles have since then become a mustard yellow. I believe it is time for a deep cleaning: one to wash away all this build up dirt and another to make me anew.

But if this was an ocean, I am sure this is the part where the sirens would have me. I would hear the call in their song sweetening me over. Their flashing scales in the water shining in different colors enticing me like a raccoon towards silver. I would reach out as they reached for me too in anticipation of my arrival. Little did I know, it would become my departure too.

I would be taken by overwhelming sensation. My breathing would get heavier. My toes then my legs, my stomach, chest, and arms would all succumb to the heat holding me in place. Slowly but surely, I would become trapped under their spell, surrendering to the relaxation the hot water provided. I would become so drowsy, lulled to the tune of its song and the heat, that I would long to fully submerge myself, fall asleep, and never wake up again.

Perhaps then, I would have some peace of mind.

AN ITCH TO SCRATCH ♉

I have an urge to write and create a physical copy of my lamentations—to feel my body in the ripples of turned pages. I want to feel myself in vellum, to put emotions in tangible form and have them exist outside of myself—in a time and space that is limitless, as memories and feelings often are.

One may find me praying to the Cosmos in the mornings and whispering my dreams in secret. Sometimes, I'd say them out loud for anyone to hear. Sometimes, I am subtle and only write a single line. Other times, I am brash and build an altar of fire so every page burns as a sacrifice and is carried off by the wind. I would scream, "These are my intentions! Do with them what thy will, sweet wind! Take them with thee and birth new life," all without ever opening my mouth.

However, some mornings are too rough to dedicate a practice to. I wake up in a fog and put off my dedication to the muse; and I'd do it again the next day until the days turn into more days, and all I have to offer are mere remnants of words—a blank page with only a ghost of letters that are merely conceived of but never actualized.

Whenever I delay the call, I beat myself up. *Don't I*

want this? Don't I want to be inspired and live a life devoted to inspiration? If yes, why do I act in opposition to my dreams?

But despite my defiance, the muse has never forsaken me as it still calls from out in the distance—banging on a stretched canopy of stars over a barrel made from a meteorite. The thumps are so distant that if I wasn't quiet, I could miss them, but once I did catch wind of them, they would only get louder and louder until they took hold of me, and the only thing left to do was run.

I'd run for my laptop and begin typing away, spewing whatever words until they coherently danced into a song worth singing. Paulo Coelho's words rang out in my ear: "If you want something, all the Universe will conspire in helping you achieve it."

Striving to meet the Universe half-way is a struggle, but on the days you manage it, even if it takes longer than you'd like, the Universe will not abandon you. It will continue to reach back if you keep on reaching, and it will reward you even if your progress is slow, as is my case with only a few words written onto a page at a time. That is the power of magic—to give in to the spell from whence it came and live by it. Magic does not care if the gradual buildup of neglect transforms your work into a barren wasteland, but only that you return and finish what you started, thus bringing life to your creation.

The Universe believes as much as you believe. Magic is half believing and half doing, and when one acts and begins scratching their itch, magic will be made.

I am only interested in conspiring with the Universe. The Universe feeds me to the point that I am satiated, *if even only for a moment.* Growing full from the cup of inspiration never lasts long—and that is a price I must pay as a writer. Another burst of inertia is needed every so often to do the trick, but the muse does not wilt so long as the itch is there, and so is its calling, reeling you back home when you answer it.

IN THE UNDERWORLD ♏︎

It is easy to say that I will not think about him. It is easy to do so during the day when I'm distracted by the perfect hairstyle, shirt to match my blue jeans and Converse, and trying to catch the A train on time to make it to my 8 a.m. class. It is easier still to forget him between Criminal Studies lectures on shotgun gauges, blood splatter trajectory, and the mindfulness of a killer. It is even easier to forget him while meeting with friends during lunch and chatting about the semester's choice of underqualified professors, who were always late and barely read any of our ten-page papers.

But I would still catch myself slipping in Literature class while reading Greek poetics of victory, tragedy, and love. Notably Icarus' plight resonates with me— an ambition so catastrophic that I've personally come to know it all too well, for I too flew too close to the sun. Even the tale of Aeneas, despite the defeat of the Trojans, strikes a chord. I often imagine how I may too triumph against the odds and sail away to an unfounded city to build a worthy empire.

One myth, however, the abduction of Persephone, pricks me harder than the others for I too have descended past daylight into a Stockholm syndrome dance with the dark.

When the sun shines above, I am granted reprieve from his constant invasion in my thoughts but later in the evenings, visions of him become hard to resist.

In a skeletal horse drawn carriage, he snatches me to meet Death under the moon. I am to relive the same story of our affair on a loop and each time I try to prevent my own downfall to no avail. I dream of running through a field of hyacinths and black roses, the ground breaking, then of a game of cat and mouse—predator and prey. Taunting and toying.

In a fell swoop, I surpass the river Styx and awake in a bed. It is dark except for a dim bluish light illuminating the room. As if he were Hades, the God of the Dead, he lies beside me and holds me close within his arms. Feeling comfort in his body heat, I would gradually relax into them and begin to feel at ease and safe; but soon after my body would shiver when he leans in for a kiss. His lips make their way to my lips then to my neck and down my shoulders. His touch is enough for me to become drunk, and I begin to feel an onset of paralysis as his true intentions dawn on me.

In a gentle yet swift movement, he pulls off my blouse and kisses my stomach. I feel the warmth of his every exhale around my navel and the peach fuzz on my skin stand straight in awe. The temperature of the room grows hotter when he unbuttons my pants and pulls them off to the side. In the middle of this bed, I lay in my undergarments.

He positions himself above me, radiating like the God that he is, and there's nothing else I want equally as badly. But by the time I catch myself giving into his whim, it is already too late. His bright green eyes fade into black, becoming vacant and dead. His touch becomes cold. His skin is icy and pale. By this point, he knows that I caught a whiff of his games. He gets up from the bed, looks down at me as I lay there almost naked, and laughs. It is deep and guttural. His eyes beam upon me, and he turns away still laughing. Echoes of his laughter continuously rings louder until he disappears out of sight.

With tears streaming down my face, I am left on the bed indisposed and disposable once again.

These nightmares jolt me awake. If I am lucky, it is already morning by the time my alarm goes off, but I still have no choice except to go on with the day exhausted from the night's dreams. Most times, I do lay awake at midnight unable to fall back asleep. I'd spent the minutes crying into my pillow, crying into the void, and crying into the dead of night until, like the dead, I too walk around hunched over with deep gray circles around my eyes the next morning.

After ingesting Hades' pomegranate seeds, I am doomed to revisit him and live by his terms for six hours a day—in my case, at night.

Despite the pain of the unchanging narrative, a part of me still looks forward to sleep. Whatever spell he had conjured has taken a hold on me. By closing the door on him in the real world, dreams have become the only time I can see and feel him again. Though his intentions have become a mockery of my devotion, a part of me still wished he sought after me and meant it. So, I'd settle for him in nightmares.

Come nightfall, my dreams reveal to me who I most desire and like clockwork it would also take it away. The maddening cycle of being led then misled is a sort of punishment made up only in the pits of this world, his world: the Underworld. It is a subjugation of Sisyphean torture for thinking I was on equal footing with the Gods. *Who was I to think that because I was captured by an Underworldly love that I too ruled here?*

Little did I understand that in arousing me from sleep, my subconscious was, in its way, warning me; wake me not from the onslaught of this nightmare, but to officially aid in shaking him off and ignite instead a power brought only by my adventures in the dark.

In truth I fell for Hades, a man with many flaws and teeth sharp enough to kill. Even though I break under his embrace, I am not broken. In his attempt to drown me in my sleep, I am each night reborn. I navigate my way into the depths, use ghosts as my

guide, and turn whatever tears fall into ammo.
With the little strength I can muster, I am reclaiming
the night as my home. These nightmares slowly
become dreams I welcome. I build walls and erect a
throne. A surge of lightning powers my veins by the
grace of the inherent divinity within me—the divinity
he tried to squander, and soon enough his visits
become less frequent.

Instead of allowing the darkness to consume me, I
am growing comfortable in it. I am yearning to
welcome it and straddle alongside the light, and I'm
sure now that I contain more life than he could ever
handle.

OCCAM'S RAZOR♏

There were days I wished for the nightmares.

I wished for the onset of sleep paralysis where my demons would come out to suffocate me in the middle of the night. I would scream inside for help yet on the outside I was silent. I would dream of being swallowed by the void and it would spit me out into a burning forest in winter. The ground and the sky, all white with snow, yet the trees burned with a fury I only felt inside. A cackling laughter, a hag, a slim body with no distinguishable eyes or mouth, and long fingernails.

Whoever they were, whatever they were, they waited for me until I fell asleep. Still after spending the night sweating under pounds of blankets and quilts for protection and praying for a rescue, I'd also wish for nightmares.

The nightmares were nothing. They did not compare to being awake and experiencing the real thing prowling behind now that you are gone.

CYCLICAL ♉

I go through cycles as easily as laundered clothes. I am tired and worn. I haven't showered in days, and I haven't left the house. My eyes are smudged with mascara and my eyeliner has crusted at the corner of my lids from not washing my face. My hair is oily and remains tied in a frizzy bun. I have decided it is better to leave it this way. My sleeves have also hardened from the mucus I've continuously wiped from my runny nose.

It is almost as if winter came by unannounced in me and in many ways, it has—except my tears have yet to turn to snow. Somehow, I am still blanketed in the cold and the draft has not gotten any better despite the windows being closed.

It is easy for me to come undone. This mess has now become familiar. This mess I live in has become my comfort.

When distractions make their way towards me, they take hold and attempt to perform an exorcism. Like a Fairy Godmother, they conjure up courage in me. Her bewitching mice detangle the strands of my hair, they scrub off the dirt from my knees, and apply blush to my pale cheeks. By the flick of her wand, Godmother summons adornments for my body, an outfit that disguises that I am falling apart. To the unsuspecting, their magic shouts confidently that "I am well put together;" though this fleshy jigsaw puzzle still has crucial missing pieces despite their efforts.

But as easily as distractions find me, they also leave. They come and go and when they retire, I must retire too. I must come home, loosen my hair band, and wring out the day from my clothes. I must close the door behind me and meet myself as I am.

Oh, what simple pleasures unfold when Godmother gifts me with distractions, but from my hands they often slip. Like a balloon, they dance upwards away from my grasp, drifting off into space and leaving me how I found myself not too long ago. The darkness creeps in when I'm alone. Godmother's charms do not work then.

Since he has been gone, I am left to sleep with demons again. They waltz throughout my bed like they have been trained to do for so many nights now, and I lay there lost within the folds of the blanket welcoming their ensemble. They have made a home within me whether I protest or not.

Soon enough dawn surely comes, and the sun rises to offer some reprieve. Light comes shining through the blinds and I meet the morning, yet again. Laying heartache to rest, the ice caps in my chest melt in the sun. Lavender flowers bloom, offerings for peace, and bright sunflowers remind me that I have not been forgotten.

The natural world has a lot to teach us. The sun rises and the sun sets. The moon waxes and it wanes. Seasons stabilize and they change. Leaves grow into a rich green and they too wither and fall away. It gets colder—but one day, it will be warmer.

Life will have its way with us. Even when we forget to wash our face and comb the knots from our hair, we are not forgotten. When the night comes as it did before and we are plagued with forgetting and remembering, please hold true that the day will bring light once more.

Even when nothing else is certain, we can be certain that this too shall pass.

Things are bound to get better again.

LIKE WHEN I WAS LITTLE ♉

When I woke up this morning, I was all alone.

"Max!" I yelled out to my dog. "Max come here!"
Usually, I would hear his little golden paws on the
wooden floor making his way towards me when I
called out his name, and then see his terrier snout
pointing in my direction as he entered my bedroom;
but instead, this morning was still. I then called out
for my mother, and she too was nowhere to be found.
I had forgotten she made plans to take Max to the
groomers this morning thus leaving me,
unbeknownst to her, in solitude with my thoughts.

I looked around my room, breathed in and let out a
heavy sigh; and immediately after, tears began to fall.
I cried for the reasons I made a wretched home out of
a broken heart—my bed is a cocoon with cheesy chip
stains on its sheets, and empty pints of vanilla ice
cream cover the bedstand. I cried for the fact that I
was desolate, and in all the ways my heart struggled
to swim across what felt like a vast dark ocean. I
could not keep the tears from coming.

This bedroom of mine was used to seeing me this
way. Every morning and night it coddled me, and the
mascara stains on my pillows was evidence of my
unraveling. In what felt like hours, I serenaded my

laments with a cocktail of devotion and self-pity with every tear. *If love is not real, then why do I hurt this bad?* I contemplated, and the tears overflowed; blinding me and making it impossible for me to navigate out of this storm.

Soon enough, I was interrupted by the opening of the front door. I heard Max's little thumps on the floor making his way to me. In a quick motion I crawled under the covers into the fetal position and hid from my mother who was sure to follow soon after. Although she had seen me distraught and disheveled before, I could not bear for her to see it all again. I felt like a failure in her eyes. I was the fool who fell for a boy and got herself in trouble again.

It didn't take her long to find me. "What's wrong?" she asked, seeing a big mass under the sheets of my bed. Still hoping that she could not see me despite how silly my attempts were to hide, I did not answer. She walked towards the bed, lifted the covers, and looked straight into my bloodshot eyes. My purple lips quivered. She let out a sigh and sat down next to me. Her hands caressed my hair.

"Come here, mama... Let's give you a bath. Let's wash your hair like when you were little," she said. Feeling like there was nothing left to do, I gave in. With all my strength, I slowly got up and followed her to the bathroom. I sat inside the tub and the running water filled it up. My mother gathered the water with a plastic Tupperware and poured it over my head, soaking my hair.

I managed to catch a glimpse of her eyes and it made me feel worse. My mother was like a mirror. The look in her eyes, tired and sunken too, reflected my feelings, and like clockwork I began to cry again.

"I'm sorry I couldn't protect you..." she began to say. "I love you. We all love you, but I guess that doesn't help, does it? Only you know what you're going through."

My mouth still could not let out a word. My throat was too sore to talk, and I feared what would come out if I did. I was afraid to expose her to the thoughts that raced through my mind and share with her the unbearable feeling in my chest. I wanted to protect her from hurting too. There was enough anguish in this house as it was.

As she continued to shampoo my head, I tried to remember the last time she washed my hair. In fact, I couldn't remember the last time at all. Most likely it involved dolls and plastic toys in the tub too. Sitting there and enjoying the heat of the water did make me recall, however, my mother's love for me. In the middle of this stormy weather, I'd forgotten that I meant something to someone, anyone other than him. I began to reminisce about the old days when it was just my mother and me. When we would play together and sleep together. At the time, she was my everything, but as I grew older, other things took her place as more important.

I cried even more on how simpler things used to be and how complicated they have all become. I wholeheartedly wanted to be okay. I wanted to be carefree and happy like the way I used to be sitting in this bathtub surrounded by bubbles and toys. I yearned to go back and bring forth a sliver of ignorance. Have it wash over me and envelop me in the only love that ever truly mattered. The love between a mother and her daughter.

She finished rinsing my hair and grabbed a warm towel fresh out of the laundry. In it she wrapped me and held me close. I could hear her heart beating. She smelled of heliotrope and vetiver. In her arms, I was no longer the same girl that entered the bathtub moments prior. Remnants of that girl swirled with the suds down the drain.

In her arms, I finally felt safe. I was protected and loved like when I was little, and everything felt like it would finally be okay.

REFLECTIONS IN THE MIRROR ♉

I have written about heartbreak ever since I can remember. It is crazy to think that even as a young girl, my first diary entry at the age of eight began with me being interested in love. I guess I am much like my father in that way, seeking for someone to fulfill the emptiness. Unlike him, however, I always stay past my welcome.

"Sometimes we have to leave when things get sour," my father said once during a car ride home. *If only it was that easy*, I thought. I had, after all, devoted my efforts in trying to build a relationship that didn't crumble when tested, and somehow, I still ended up sorting through the rubble.

"I am a firm believer of love," he said. "It is just hard. In a relationship, sacrifices must be made to make the relationship work, and even then, sacrifices may not be enough."

I looked up at him. His big brown eyes and button nose are reflected in me. Among his looks, I also have inherited his sense of humor, making everyone feel at ease through laughter. He cares about the world, and he inspires me to travel to see more of it. We have seen the ends of the earth together: hiking through the ruins in Rome, riding Tuk Tuks in Siem Reap, advocating for human rights in New York. Though my father could be heartless on days he feels wronged, I have never met another with as much compassion for humanity as him. *With his big heart, why is it that he has yet to settle down?* I wondered.

As a little girl, I used to witness his magic. His voice would drop a little, he'd lean in closer, and spoke with much suave. Every time he made the girls laugh and they quickly took a liking to him. On a few occasions, I've discovered various love letters with his signature. He talked about love like poets did and reading his words I understood from where the lover in me was born.

"I haven't found the *right* one," he continued. "So, I'm going to keep trying until I *find* the right one."

I can see in his eyes all the pain he has ever felt when in love. He never suppressed his sentimental nature in front of me, which opposed my mother's narrative. "He is so irresponsible," she would say. "He is cold and always acts before thinking, and often screws everything up." But quite often I did see him cry like when thinking of his mother, when recalling his last love, and while watching *The Little Princess*.

"Love is overrated, and only makes you do dumb things and hurt people," my mother said. I didn't bat an eye when she spoke of him like that then. As a child, I tried my best not to meddle into the affairs of adults but look at me now; entangled in the complexities of adult emotions. I felt betrayed like my mother, but I also felt optimistic like my father. *Do I keep searching too, or do I abandon ship?*

If only it was that simple to believe as my father does—to continue searching until love decides to stay forever. If only I had the same unwavering courage to join the search for the *right one*. But *what was there to search for when I thought I had already found the one?*

He turned on the radio and began to bellow a song about unrequited love. The singer's voice was somber, yet hopeful. My dad's fingers danced with the cadence of the lyrics in the air like an orchestra conductor, and he kept on singing. A lump made its way in my throat then and tears gathered in the corner of my eyes as I listened in silence. *Is the right one really out there?* I considered.

As I contemplate my father's words and the radio, my broken heart weaves them into a prayer directed towards the deities of love, whomever they may be. I need them to know that we are reaching, and in turn, that they respond by reaching back.

TOO GOOD TO BE TRUE ♉

I learned to convince myself
just about anything.

That I am fine.

That I am okay.

That I can move on.

I begin to believe it all since believing
is all I could do
to keep from toppling   over.

I move forward no matter how much
The past wants to catch up to me,

            and it all works for a while

Until a song plays on the radio or
a romance begins at the end of a commercial.

If I am not careful, I could be left
without distractions.

I could be left with a montage of
painful flashbacks and unrestrained emotions

If I am not careful,
I could be so taken aback.

I could crack open in mid-   thought.
I could break in the flesh
and bleed from the seams

LOOSE KNOTS ♏

Sometimes I wonder whether it was really
supposed to be this way.

All that hard work we had done;
All that progress we made;
All the tears we shared;
All in our unraveling.

Were all those promises meant to break?

Were we meant to let go twice before
to make this time our last?

Will I enjoy music again and get used
to dancing on my own?

Will these tear ducts ever run dry?

Was this really supposed to happen?

Were we really supposed to end this way?

Will I make it out alive this time?

SATURDAY MORNINGS ♏

On Saturday mornings you used to come over bright and early as if we both rolled out of bed together moments prior. You'd bring milk, eggs, and bread. I already had cinnamon and the vanilla extract.

"No, that's not the way you do it," you would say, snatching the mixture of milk and eggs from my hands. We would always fight during our Saturday morning ritual of making French toast. I eyeballed measurements while your traditions fought hard to stick to defined recipes. No deviations were allowed.

To enjoy the making of our meal, I decided not to push my luck and tasked myself with buttering the pan and watching over the toast till each side reached that perfect shade of golden brown.

In hindsight, our relationship was a host of metaphorical French toasts. The milk could have soured if we did not take notice. We eat shells if we crack the eggs too hard in our bowl. The bread could fall apart if we dredge it in milk for too long. The toast would burn if we were not vigilant. Even the dressing of maple syrup would fail in saving the mess we create.

Now waking up on Saturday mornings, I wonder if it

was all a dream. Whether the smell of nutmeg was only a figment of my imagination. Looking around the kitchen now, I see the memory of both of us laughing before me. As you whisk the eggs, you give me that look—the one that makes my cheeks flush, and I'd become hot in all types of places. I hand you the gallon of milk as an agreement to your advances, and French toast would become secondary to what we were *actually* cooking in the kitchen thereafter.

I stare ahead from my seat in the kitchen island, and shortly the ghosts of our relationship fade before my eyes taking the laughter with it. The kitchen becomes quiet once more, and I am left to complete the Saturday morning ritual by myself this time.

UNFAMILIAR ♏

I look through all the pictures we have ever taken together and mostly they are of you. I have you scattered all over my room in scrapbooks, frames, and photo boxes. Your face, our embrace, and your kisses are everywhere. Even certain photographs are inscribed into my memories like the one with you as a baby at the beach with a blue hat and your face tilted towards the sun like a heliotrope, or the one with you wearing glasses holding Max as a mummy on Halloween. I don't know why, but Max took a liking to you from the start. He allowed you to hold him and make him dance while others cowered at his growl.

When looking at these photographs and paying close attention to the faces you made, the face I grew to love (or so I thought), I found myself asking, "Who is this boy? Did I really know him?" I don't recall our meeting, but a version of myself must have been smitten because now I have no clue nor memory of what led me to you.

These photographs now have an eerie quality to them, almost like encountering a distorted reflection of yourself in a house of mirrors. You enter in with a strong sense of your identity, but as you study the images before you, you start to question who you really are. *Is this person before me a familiar friend or foreign foe?* I cannot recall a time when I looked at these photos that lay before me now and felt differently. Even though I am pictured hugging, smiling, and kissing you, it all feels so distant and nostalgic, almost unreal.

I am beginning to think you were a figment of my imagination all along because you are nothing but a mere stranger now.

A BIG ADVENTURE ♉

To die would be an awfully big adventure—or so I think as I look death in the face as an adventurous child does when battling existential enemies: ticking crocodiles, a pirate with a hook for a hand, a broken heart, and the like.

I now find myself questioning my existence and the ceasing thereof. I hold the tools in my hands and savor the blade there. I look it over from side to side and shift its weight between my fingers. It isn't smooth like a kitchen knife nor as shiny, but maybe it will do. As I sit at the edge of my bed naked and press the blade to my skin, a sudden thought comes to mind: "This will get messy." After all, the blade is rusty and now I am worried of the potential lock jaw and tight muscle spasms I could endure if I caught tetanus instead.

My dog barked in the distance. *Who would walk him when I'm gone? What about my mother? Would she die of a broken heart too?*

I think of tomorrow and the lack of certainty that comes with it. This is not something I really want to do, but rather, I feel *compelled* to. Sorrow does that to you. It's a siren who calls your name and lures you deeper until there is no escaping their grasp. Sorrow plays tricks and makes you think they love you but urges you to submit. Maybe it is out of love or pity as an act to put me out of my misery, or perhaps Sorrow has a taste for theatrics and yearns to capture their latest victim in any way possible.

Sorrow came to me like a maiden in the night amid a fever dream. She extends a hand to me now and urges that I continue what I started as a cure all. I look up at her, a black shadowy figure before me. "No," I whispered, even hesitantly. I may not know what tomorrow brings, but what I do know is that despite all the heaviness I feel in my bones and in my heart, at this moment I do not want to die.

My Spirit within said, "Not now. Not this way," and here with the Angel of Death lingering by for a kiss, I decided I wanted to live. Although I wish for the hurt to go away, I also longed for the possibilities of what may come next:

Adventures across the Atlantic ocean; cuddling a tiny ball of fluff with a wet nose on cold nights; staying up late to catch the moon at its fullest in August; singing out loud to my favorite artist, Bad Bunny, in concert; having my first hot cup of chai tea during a layover in Texas; encountering rainbows everywhere every time I least expect it, but need it; finding a community madly in love with magic and tarot as much as I am; spending a decade laughing over hard ciders and wine with my best friend; and holding a beautiful child with curly hair and almond eyes like mines.

So, it must be true then that to *live* would be an awfully big adventure too.

THIS IS A SPILL, THIS IS A SPELL ♉

This is a spell both literally and metaphorically.

In these times of sadness and grief, I am not myself, yet the symptoms that are so totally and utterly unrecognizable are completely my own. They were birthed from a place of longing and need, and despite the entanglement my heart finds itself in, they have become an ushering that stirs me into a place of comfort—into a field of poppies that welcome sleep for the wandering soul. A soul like mine that seeks endlessly for a reprieve, even that of eternal sleep.

This unearthing is the kind of spell that renders you oblivious to the world as if you have called down angels themselves to rock you gently to sleep to end the many sleepless nights. Out of pity for your cries, the angels do come and bring Baby's Breath, both as a sacred offering and for mourning.

These words I write are the same—a symptom of an ego collapsed, and a heart broken wide open. It is a spell like an undercurrent that has rewired me to strictly feel—and feel is all I can do. It seems I became more Cancerian in nature than level-headed— more water than earth, and muddier in-between.

I look back and read the words written during this cold and I am taken aback by the Hyde of sorts that made itself known across the lined pages—a shadow projected in keystrokes and allowed to run amuck on a white page.

This is not me, I think. *But isn't it me?* Aren't I the same person who spun words that healed as much as they strangled?

Aren't these words a spill? A dam broken free. It's drops of water searching for its ocean home and it's leaking all the complexities that resides in me.

Aren't these words a mirror? A portal to another realm that is of my reflection, but not quite this reality.

Whatever this is, this isn't. Whatever this isn't, this is.

A STATE OF TRANSITION

SPIN ♉

During the summers of the late 90s, my grandparents used to drive an hour out to Coney Island. In the back seat of their old school Ford van were their children, my aunt and uncle, and I was squeezed between them. My aunt and uncle were close to my age, and they treated me like a younger sibling rather than their niece which meant I was often adored as the "cute one" but I was also made easy pickings for my uncle's frequent pestering.

As we neared the beach boardwalk after our hour-long car ride, my eyes would grow wide in amazement. I'd push my way to the car window and with my head out I'd smell popcorn and funnel cake in the air. In the distance, I could hear screams and laughter of both terrified and happy children all around. Neon lights blinked from the amusement park as prizes were won. Strengths were tested with a softball like texture hammer hitting a gong with a loud thud.

"Look at them all!" I squealed. "I'm going to go on all the rides!" and I pointed towards the bumper cars, then the Wonder Wheel, then the Cyclone.

"That's if they let you on. You're too little," my uncle said and pinched my arm.

"Stop that!" I yelled. "I'm a big kid, of course they will let me on!" I was determined to be adventurous.

Once out of the car, we all made our way through the crowds. There were cheers and loud music. The crashing of the waves could also be heard, and the sea salt breeze began to frizz my curls.

"Oh, Christie! Look at this ride," my grandma said and gently pulled me towards the direction to my first attraction of the night. "Go on, go ahead," she said. "I'll be right here."

My aunt and uncle stayed behind. "Aren't you coming?" I asked.

"No, we are too old for *that* ride!" They said shaking their head and scurried off.

I turned back and faced the ride. Small and anxious children all made their way before me. Some with their parents, others on their own. I followed suit and hesitantly opened the small white door to an empty oversized teacup all for myself. I climbed in and sat in the middle. *What happens now?* I thought. I see the other children grab hold onto the black metal steering wheel in the middle of the teacup and I too did the same. The conductor queued the music which mimicked the sounds of a carousel, and the floor beneath me slowly started to move.

I braced myself and held onto the wheel in front of me, but it gave way to spinning in place, and I too began to spin. I went along and continued to turn the wheel, and my teacup spun faster and faster. Round and round I went and met each time where I first started. My hair danced out of control as the wind whooshed through it.

Emotions ran through me. I was excited, but then scared as the speed of the tracks below me picked up its pace and the lights around me became all a blur. I no longer could distinguish my grandma's face from the bystanders in the crowd. Everyone sounded the same. It was all laughter and all cries as all the children in their own teacups shrieked with joy and with fear. Then I grew dizzy and attempted to slow the turn of the wheel, but no matter my attempts, I was held hostage to the tracks below that also spun on their own.

Soon enough, my teacup started to slow down, and the music's volume lowered. I could somewhat begin to distinguish the faces around me. My heart raced despite reaching a complete stop, and my knees wobbled as I made my way out of the teacup back to the crowd.

"Christie, over here!" My grandma yelled. I ran to her and hugged her for dear life. She clutched me in her arms laughing. "You're really dizzy, huh?" She said, and we slowly walked off to find the others.

I felt nauseous, yet giddy as if butterflies had also circled in my stomach too. I couldn't tell whether I was sick or thrilled of the spinning teacups; but what was certain was that I could be found making my way back to those teacups, going through the same motions, for every summer thereafter.

Much like falling in love and much like falling out of it.

EXES WITH BENEFITS ♍

My first love was a lanky kid with a head full of hair spiked up at the front who was perpetually wearing something from American Eagle. His jeans were always tight, and they hugged his bony frame. He smelled of Axe body spray and Irish Springs. He was neat and clean and to me that was important. At the time, I saw him as my everything, but I've come to learn that even everything can be replaceable.

I didn't know how to kiss, but he taught me under the trees of Franklin D. Roosevelt Park. My lips would follow his for hours until my mother grew worried and called for me to come home. Although I would come home to a lecture, I would find myself back again with him the next day. A bench at the park became our spot and even to this day, I cannot drive past it without thinking of what became of him.

We thought we gave it all we had our first time together, but life proved to us that we weren't done. Not yet anyways, for it granted us a chance to heal new wounds by revisiting and making love to the old. So, within this new battleground I found myself fighting in, I leaned into him to nurse me back to health.

We were familiar, and we searched within the heat of

one another for comfort to fill in the spaces that were void. I felt abandoned and broken for so long that in his touch I found sentiments of love and pleasure and in me, he was no longer lonely. We stayed up talking on the phone like before, getting to know each other for what seemed like the first time, and we called each other "babe" as if we meant it.

We were with one another in secret, but never belonged to each other; and with every escapade we took advantage of, we grew more confident. The fire within us burning again. I too began to laugh once more. I had almost forgotten what it was like to find joy and have it sit with you without asking for anything in return. The things that used to tick us off about each other like his self-pity and crappy friends, and my clinginess and need of validation meant nothing since unconditional love did not exist here— we did not have to accept each other's flaws this time.

We became mere vessels for one another's sadness. Where he looked for himself in between my moans and crevices, I looked for another in his eyes and touch. The passion that lacked our first time around became intense and swift, and left us asking for more every time. We became experts of making love to each other without being *in* love. Within time, we instantly felt better even though we knew that *whatever* we had created wasn't going to last. We were just using each other until the next best thing.

Despite feeling satisfied, my first love and I were still left to face our own battles whenever we parted. The moment he would leave, my world would become quiet and dim again. Looking back, he was only here to help turn on the lights.

We were distractions to each other and that was all we could ever be.

DIAMONDS MAY NOT BE
SO PRECIOUS AFTER ALL ♉

Looking back, I wonder whether I started equating love with tears and this became an unconscious theme that I perpetuated throughout my relationships.

The first time I saw a boy cry and beg for me to stay was the moment that I made a dangerous connection. I thought to myself, *if they aren't willing to die for me, they truly did not love me.* In mathematical terms:

$$if\ (\text{``hurt''}\ is\ at\ or\ greater\ than\ X) +$$
$$(Y\ in\ relationship) = true\ love$$

$$X = limit/maximum,\ Y = time$$

If X and Y stayed constant, the results validated my worthiness. Whatever consequences came from almost break-ups like distrust, fear, or alienation was worth it, like the way a diamond could only grow under pressure, except this time the pressure was built by tears.

What a sadistic venture I had tapped into at the age of sixteen.

LOST GIRL FOUND ♉

One would know how deep in trouble I was by the number of books I read cover to cover in a week.

"Can we stop by the bookstore before we get home?" I would ask my parents. My stepdad would sigh. *Books cost money*, he thought, since he paid for them, and I was sure to leave with about five to six books in one trip. "You take forever in there," my mom would say and frown as she began to reminisce about a child she used to understand.

When I read, I did not have time for my own thoughts or my own words. I would become distracted with the boy with the lightning scar off to wizardly adventures and live out between the pages of heroines and mystery plots. I would sleuth with the best teenage girl detective, but also long to never grow up and be taken to a land far away like Peter Pan did with Wendy.

If he comes for me, we would soar the night sky of the city, fly over the Empire State building, find that second star to the right, and fly on straight till morning. I would roam deep in the forests, smear dirt under my eyes, disguise myself in leaves so I would not fall trap to Hook's ways. I would be so far from home, one might call me "lost"—but even then, I'm sure I would not fit in at Neverland for long. Peter thought girls too clever to ever lose their way like his boys.

Yet, I *was* lost—yet I didn't mind, because the farther I read and the more pages I turned, the farther from this reality I became. No one understood except for the characters in my books. They would reach out their hand through the seams and pull me into their portal.

Book by book, I would stack them as I read them all, moving on from one to the next. Chapter after chapter, story after story, portal after portal. I would conjure a world in color where mine was dulling to gray. I admired the words inked onto the cream-colored pages by creatives who also searched for something more—authors who dreamt in color too and perhaps were seeking refuge from a world of their own.

It was in their words and in their stories that I instead was found. Even though I may have been running all this time, the writers that I've long admired gifted me with the power of imagination— equipping me with the weapon to reclaim my own story and defeat my own hook-handed pirate too.

THE WHEEL OF FORTUNE♏

I have fallen for your John Cusack ways serenading me outside my window.

It had been about a year since we last spoke and many core memories have been made since then: new friendships, a new prom date, high school graduation came and went, and college was just around the corner.

Without the distraction of school, you were enticed to search for me again. It was the season when the blades of grass have held us throughout the summer nights and, like the year before, the Hudson River witnessed the first of our many kisses during its sunsets. Although running away should have been the thing I did when I found you throwing stones at my window, I instead met you as if you had never left. Immediately and beyond my control, I became the same little girl at the playground those many years ago. This part was Act I.

Looking back, did you target me from the beginning? Did you know that I would be the one to fall trap to your games? Did you know that I would lose my head over you?

You were "it" then and cornered me under the metal

slides of our elementary school playground. It was our first time playing with one another during recess. For months now, we have been eyeing each other without ever saying a word. Every day you played soccer at the other end of the field, while I could be found playing freeze tag with friends. On this day, you trekked from your side of play and crossed into mine, wanting to "tag" too.

Under the slides, you reached out your hand to tag me and in that moment time slowed down. Echoes of pre-pubescent laughter rang in our ears, and we locked eyes. The hair on my skin raised in anticipation for your touch, while the rhythm of your chest moved up and down from the chase. Your eyes, bright and blue, matched your polo-shirt and I was utterly and completely smitten in an instant.

"I gotcha," you said, and smirked. Little did I know how true that statement would be for the nine years thereafter. Your hand touched my arm, freezing me in place and you ran off. Although that was the objective of the game, I was paralyzed by the effect you had on me. Unbeknownst to me, summer was yet to fully unfold, and I'd be falling for you and breaking apart over and over again.

The school bell rang calling us all to return inside for class. That bell. What a harbinger of chaos. It tried to warn me, to wake me up from your spell and prevent a relationship doomed from the start. Instead, I did not listen and now find myself in bed grieving us for the third time. Yet, I cannot get over how you pursued me that day in the school yard. Much like how you begged to be let in outside my window and left apologies in voicemails. Now this was the beginning of Act III.

That time, you started the wheel once more by sending a message. I had hoped that you would have come to realize the error in your ways sooner. My heart had closed off any possibilities for reconciliation to preserve what little sanity you had left me with. This was the aftermath of our Act II.

"I've come to realize that after all this time, I still love you," your message read, "I had repressed whatever feelings I had and for that I am sorry. I still want you..."

Then you proceeded to bombard me with quotes of forgiveness and etched my name onto your skin with a knife as a display of your martyrdom.

"I'd do anything," you said, and you wouldn't stop knowing that I, truth be told, did not want you to. You were ravenous and sought me like a meal, and kept on until I gave in. I surrendered to you once more, befalling that same fate in the playground. You reignited the black flame candle bringing us back from the dead because despite everything, I still loved you and you played that to your advantage.

I then had pulled the same tricks as we neared the end of Act III. With the tables turned, I reenacted the play in the same manner you led it. I pushed and pulled you close, manipulating you in my hands till I was finally able to unfreeze the hold you had on me.

Though I'm no heroine, it was time I ended our tragedy for good.

DRUNKEN NIGHTS ♌

After the fifth shot everything felt great. I had all the energy to dance and talk, and perhaps even run laps. My friends were as drunk as I was, and the night was still young. Though it was only ten on a Friday night it felt like the hour of the wolf. The moon's shone brightly through the windows.

Despite being surrounded by people, I still felt lonely. I snuck off to the terrace and leaned over the railing to watch the folks below me; or rather, I hoped I would catch a glance of a familiar face. *What I wouldn't do to see that face again...* Looking down at the streets, everything looked tiny. At this time of night, the streets were desolate except for the few making their way home from SoHo and the dogs out for a late-night bathroom run, and everything else in between was blurry—a side effect from all the vodka I'd ingested prior.

While standing at the railing, I thought, *if I were to fall right here, right now, the fall would be painful even if only for a moment. But perhaps it would all get better then.*

I looked up and was met with the stare of the moon, the same moon who has heard the wailing of the widows and the lonely banshees wishing on a star for their lovers to return. The ones they would call hysterical. People like me. This is the same moon who witnessed others jump before it into a blurry sea like the one beneath me now. Those who jumped far deeper in love than they had hoped. The ones they would call crazy. People like me.

My heart began to pound at the thought of what I might do. I quickly turned and rushed back inside, afraid that my intoxication may lead me to leap over the ledge without thinking further.

I was in no position to walk and with every step, I stumbled. Amid the crowd, I beelined for home when home was no longer here. I ran instead into the arms of my best friend. A boy who, like me, was madly in love, but I was too anchored to someone else to notice that who he wanted was me all along. I didn't know it then, but he would later become the one to finally show me what true unconditional love is.

He hugged me tight, and I began to cry as I've done many nights before. My nose nestled into his arms, breathing him in between each cry. The scent of sweet cocoa butter comforted me, and his soft hands were warm as he rubbed my back. Without saying so much of a word, we sat down on the couch, and he cradled me like a baby. Having been by my side these gut-wrenching months, he understood immediately what was wrong and intuitively shaped into how he could be of service.

"I don't get it," I said to him. "I didn't do anything wrong this time... I wasn't the one to push him away." The words were muffled and chaotic, but he understood, nonetheless. The tears continued to cascade. I was confused and nothing made any sense.

I then recalled the events that led to my breakup and tried to deduce meaning from the pieces. *Were there any signs? Any warnings? Was it all on me and I did not realize?* Ghosts were swimming in my head, smiling and laughing in the summer parks then some turned into stone, emotionless and cold like winter. The rest of them began spinning around me and then the whole world spun too, and I was lost in a portal I'd hoped never to be in again.

Like a gravity blanket, my best friend held me tighter the deeper I fell into the dark rabbit hole he could not see but felt. I was exhausted, and he rocked me like one would rock a child to sleep. His sunny disposition and warm embrace slowly brought me back to the present.

I couldn't change the past nor the choices that were made, and although those were two truths I did not like coming to terms with, they were the light I needed at that moment. I slowly opened my eyes and looked up at him. He had such beautiful brown and caring eyes that reminded me of a kind teddy bear. The crying had finally stopped. I sat up and wiped what was left of my tears and sighed.

I laid my head on his shoulders and held his arm in mine, and he did the same. I didn't know what would come of tomorrow, whether I'd be tempted to look over the railing once more, or whether I'd be haunted by the same ghosts. All I knew was that this right here with my dear friend was true, and I'm glad the night did not end any other way.

THIS IS A SPILL, THIS IS A SPELL PART II ♉

When I was younger, I used to be afraid of mirrors. Not of mirrors *per se*, but rather what accompanied staring into my reflection for too long. Before a bath, I would climb on top of the sink for a better look when searching for blemishes. I would sit cross-legged and stare into the mirror before me. I'd see my eyes staring back—bright, big, and almost black. I'd have to get close to the light to see the true color of my iris, a mocha brown like my father's yet sharp like my mother's. I would trace the peach fuzz on my cheeks, pull my mouth wide and examine my teeth, and expand my nostrils to consider plucking hairs.

I'd never know how I'd get here, but soon enough I'd release her. She is a reflection... so much like me—but not quite. I'd stay longer to see what she wouldn't follow as my hand waved and my eyes bounced side to side, still never losing sight of her. I'd grow tired and soon a smile would creep across her face. It was this grin that sent me running to the hills, leaving the mirror to now reflect the white ceramic tile standing before it.

But there were days she'd catch me before I had the chance to run. Her charade of keeping up with my pace was so on point that I never caught her slipping. If I had lost concentration for even a second, she would be the one to catch me. She'd whisper, "this is a spell," and lure me behind the silver metallic surface. She was a siren catching prey, and in return, she was granted freedom, leaving me instead trapped in the mirror world until she grew bored and came looking to switch planes again.

In her daring audacity, I had mistakenly unleashed a spell and opened the portal that set her free. Except for the lack of twinkle in her dead eyes, no one could spot a difference and take notice that the girl they now interacted with was taken ahold by something more insidious. She was night and I was day, and the writing under her pen now bore a contrasting tone— yet had a similar signature to my own.

To bring her back and become successful in switching planes once more, I may have to set another spell. I must create an incantation made of acceptance, love, and kindness, to create a compromise that allows her to roam until it is time to go home, to listen and to hold space for all her mess, to bring softness to the jagged edges, and to allow room for the stars to make a permanent home in her eyes returning that twinkle she had lost long ago.

Surely, the hex would be broken then.

THE "IT'S COMPLICATED" IN FRIENDSHIP ♌

You know that expression, "Love when you're ready and not when you're lonely"?

At what stage do we know when we are not ready, or rather when we are lonely? Because everything just feels so right when I'm with you even though I've promised myself to another who left a while ago.

But within your arms, I have found a comfort that I have never known before. A type of love born out of respect and reverence, and not lust or appearance. It's comforting like a steamy cheese pizza and pint of cinnamon swirl ice cream. *Is this what it's like to be into your best friend?*

We witnessed each other grow during our most pivotal and primal moments. Navigating puberty in the mess of complicated and frivolous high school drama, we worked our first paying job together earning nothing but chump change and laughs. And we spoke till sundown of scary movies and longings for more.

You've witnessed me during a time when only I confided in my writing and with care you listened, holding up my hair as I purged a version of myself out of which I was metamorphosing. You saw me in my messiness, smudged mascara, and all. You laughed when I didn't shave for months, and I joked I was growing my armpit hair long enough to swing from like a vine. You smelt the worst of farts and heard the loudest of burps. Everything that I longed to hide and conform to be the perfect girl, I've laid out in front of you bare. I've fallen asleep in your arms far quicker than I do in my own bed.

And despite how loud I could be and my willingness to act before thinking, you still choose me, and I feel it. I am drawn to you. There is an electricity that emanates when you're near and it continues to intensify when you leave.

I shouldn't complicate this friendship, but perhaps complications are what's called for when the energy between us has become palpable.

Maybe "comfort" is not a bad thing.

Maybe it is exactly the type of relationship I should be striving for.

TO PICK A ROSE ♌

After the end of *Nick and Norah's Infinite Playlist*, my best friend and I laid there looking at each other. Hurricane Sandy has left us without power for a few days now and though he had a home of his own with electricity thriving, he wanted to brave the storm with me.

My portable DVD player had enough power to last about a couple of days and we were making the most of it watching new films and old classics. *Nick and Norah* had been my pick—a not so obvious love story taking place in our home city. Considering how close we were getting lately, I figured he would have liked it too.

It was early in the night, but the leaves outside were falling and autumn had cast a tenebrous fog over the city. Paired with the fact that there was no power, the inside of the home was even darker. We lit candles to provide us with light. I felt comfortable having him there beside me in bed. The heat from his body made me feel too warm. There was a faint aroma of cocoa butter on his skin, and the scent reminded me of when my father would lather cocoa butter on my knees and elbows when I was a child—his cure-all remedy for dry skin.

It had been a while since I have been this close to a guy let alone felt love in the simple and innocent act of lying near each other. I fed him warm kisses on his lips and in the crevice of his neck. I whispered secrets into his ear. He didn't say a word and only stared back with a slight smile. His eyes would do all the talking and in it I could sense his deep affection towards me. His presence emitted a powerful energy that created a tingling sensation within my body, making me shudder.

He wants me, I thought. *This boy right here wants me. He* wants a *forever*—something I also wanted so badly I would have given everything for, but immediately a wave of regret washed over me.

Doesn't he know that he lied in bed with a monster? Doesn't he know how this is going to end?

I nervously stared into his brown eyes as they stared back into my soul. I recalled another pair of eyes— blue-green ones that pierced straight through me. Those eyes promised forever like the shine of a diamond. The holder of those eyes was who I wanted. He was who I expected to be laying here next to me, but I have come to learn that diamonds too can become matte and dull with wear.

"I'm sorry," I told him, "For playing with you, for leading you on..." I paused to take a deep breath in. "I am just so sorry..." I let out.

He took a deep sigh and took his time before answering. "It doesn't matter," he finally said, holding me tighter.

But it does matter! I screamed internally. No one should pick a rose without gloves, for the thorns alone were enough to wound.

I lingered my fingers on his cheeks and around his eyes, I closed my eyes hoping that this would have all been but a dream. I closed them even tighter, and tears streamed down my cheeks. My fingers tightened around his face.

Please, I pleaded within. *Please let this be a dream. When I open my eyes, I wish to see my lover where my best friend is now. Wake me up from this nightmare. Please? Please...*

My eagerness further drove out more tears. I felt my chest brace itself. I thought if I wished hard enough that maybe my prayers would come true. If I lied to myself hard enough that maybe such lies would become the truth.

When I lifted my lids, my heart sank. I loosened the grip on my fingers. My shoulders dropped and my soul went back into hiding. My best friend was still there in front of me.

His look grew worried. His hands grasped my arms

trying to comfort me, but I didn't need comforting. I planted a kiss on his eyes and meant it. I turned around facing my back to him and tried to fall asleep. I heard him sit up at the corner of the bed. He sat there for a while, I didn't know what for, but I felt he knew what I was thinking, that he knew he could not offer what I searched for. A knot rolled up my throat and I felt even more selfish than before. He got up and blew out the candles, and slowly walked out of my room.

Left in darkness, I whispered out "I'm sorry" one last time and wondered whether it was meant for the boy with the brown eyes or the one with blue.

THE NEXT MORNING ♌

The next morning, I woke up feeling refreshed. Though the events of last night had left me exhausted, a night's sleep was what I needed to clear my head, and this morning I was clear on one thing.

We found ourselves sitting on my bed yet again. I watched him from afar. He sat on the corner with his head down staring at his hands—his fingers rubbing the back of his knuckles. What he was searching for in them I did not know, but I was confident that he would find it once I made things up.

Making the first move, I made my way behind and wrapped my legs around him. My arms embracing him. In haste, I kissed his neck and blew hot air around his ears, and softly licked his lobes. He turned around and looked at me with hesitation. He must have been confused considering all that occurred just the night prior, but I knew then that I had to have him.

"Do you want me to stop?" I asked in a whisper.

My best friend looked me straight in the eyes. The morning's light casted a twinkle in his. "No," he exhaled.

I then exhaled loudly too and reached out to hold his chin and brought it close to mine. My eyes closed and I leaned in. His lips felt like smooth butter. His kiss pushed back into mine and then I knew that he wanted me as much as I wanted him. My hands went under his shirt and with my nails I traced circles and lines across his chest—sigils of love, passion, and protection. He let out a soft laugh and although it tickled, I knew he liked being under my spell.

In a bold attempt, I pushed him back on the bed so that I could mount and let my full weight fall upon him. His fingers became tangled in my curly hair as his hands pulled me closer. Our limbs followed suit.

I could not tell whether I was trying to make myself feel better by getting lost in his touch, but it did not matter. This morning, this calf made peace with the young lion.

Outside the New York City streets were dead, and though we were desolate and the air around us seemed still, the hurricane found its way in and grew between us stronger than before.

FRAGRANCE ♏

It was a cold winter day in SoHo and a long list of Christmas gifts led me into the first floor of Bloomingdale's perfume section. After begging to let me in on what my best friend-now-boyfriend would like to open on Christmas day, he admitted a cologne. Little did he know that I knew the exact scent he blurted out very well.

"This one please," I motioned to the woman behind the counter pointing towards the blue and white striped silhouette of a sailor. She took the bottle from under the glass casing for me to hold and test. "Oh, no worries," I said, "I know this is the one I want." The woman nodded her head, placed the tester bottle on the counter, and proceeded to shuffle through cabinets of cologne wrapped in cellophane. Staring at *Le Male's* torso with broad shoulders and all left before me, I decided to spray Jean-Paul Gaultier's signature scent on my wrist anyway. Without a moment to waste, the woman came with a pleasant, gift-wrapped box of the cologne. I handed her cash and quickly left the store thereafter.

After walking out of the department store with the cologne in a brown paper bag in hand, I was braced with a smack in the face. The scent from my wrist surprised me as I had tucked a loose hair behind my ear, and visions flashed in front of me. I walked down Broadway Street in a trance as people from all directions walked past me. Streaks of light rushed by, and memory presented me with a familiar face.

Out of the sea of people, I could vividly see *him*. His rosy cheeks spotted with freckles. His round button nose. His navy-blue beanie snuggled on his head. Immediately, I wanted to cry. It has been months since I last smelled this scent and it instantly brought me back to a place I no longer wanted to be in, but I did not mind returning.

His bright green eyes beamed ominously and his hand motioned me towards him amidst the crowd. As I walked towards him, he then began to fade. His memory began to subside as so did the scent of *Le Male* and suddenly, it was nighttime on Broadway. I blinked twice to reorient and found myself again in the middle of a busy street full of frantic strangers shopping for holiday gifts. I was on my own as before.

It is amazing how memory can be triggered by the faintest thing. Despite my efforts, *Le Male* uncovered that which I have tried to repress; and now with presents soon to be unwrapped, I'm afraid I will never get the chance to forget.

MEMORY ♉

I used to document everything.

Pictures, conversations, love songs, and quotes.

My journals are filled with monologues and dialogues, emotions and memories caught in real time. If I was not nostalgic and had the need to collect that which brings me joy or sadness, trapping the soul of a moment onto a page, I would have easily forgotten them as quickly as they came. Now, reading back and turning the pages, I can relive these moments. However, now I am the only one plagued with the burden of remembering them.

Memory is much like a sociopath. It is manipulative and deceitful, dominant at first, then gets harder to believe over time.

GHOSTS ♉

There is a strand that sticks out here. A lifeline of
sorts reaching out to grab my hand and jolt me with
remnants of what was. In this neighborhood, in this
park on this grass—I'd like to say I grew up here
nestled between the trees, and the Hudson River;
between the sprinklers of the playground, the sunset
at the marina; between the oil stained seats of the
movie theater (the first of plenty of dates); between
the buttered bagels toasted before class, the lunches
on the West Street bridge; between the lips of first
kisses, and the tears of my mother's resistance to her
child growing up; between best friends gained and
lost; between becoming and became, and laughter
and heartaches.

Though my body is still adjusting, this is home.
Though I continue to stray far away, the river
connects me. Despite the number of years that pass
by, I'm always brought back to adolescence the
moment I cross Church Street.

I worry whether the boats on the pier revolve around
me the way basketballs used to circle the rim during
practice. Whether my V-neck is low enough to show
what little breasts I had when compared to Allison's.
I worry whether I'd see that freckled boy who I loved
and hated and loved and hated, time and time again.

These remnants plague me as I witness toddlers become children become teenagers become adults on Chambers. Usually, I see ghosts of the past in the flesh; but lately, the tenants of this town are unrecognizable and here, I am remaining all the same.

The only ghost here is me.

SHADOW DANCE ♉

I have tried running away from myself more times than I could count.

I have run into other's words, their stories both mystical and real, with my nose deep in books; and I found myself being reflected there in tea-stained pages, highlighted quotes, and soliloquies.

I have tried running to lovers whose arms I wished would pick me up and twirl me around like I was the prettiest thing, but instead, I never left the ground of my own room.

I have even tried to drown myself in drinks and music, but instead, I found my own thoughts swirling within the vodka and tea infused cocktails with every sip I took. Lana Del Rey's soulful voice usually playing in the background, piercing right through me, affirming my laments, and making me nostalgic. The constant brooding melody in her music mesmerizes me, lulling deeper into a poetic slumber.

The thought of drinking in solitude during these moments did not faze me, but I did fear the dark and nebulous mass that emerged outside myself after consuming one too many libations. Without this shadowy companion conjoined at my hip, the world around me spun out of control, and the more it spiraled, the more the Shadow grew restless, wanting to let loose, and take over what little control I had.

The looming darkness shifts out of its warm, fleshy home, becoming increasingly tangible and dancing its way to chaos. Every time it loosens from my grip, my inner world reflects that of theirs. It is gloomy, erratic, and demanding; and it leaves me exposed, speaking out of turn, and giving into my intrusive thoughts.

What a flimsy, naughty thing that Shadow is. How could it be such a significant part of me, yet live outside of me, and cause such chaos?

In retrospect, without it I am lost. Regardless of how often I would look for a diversion to quell my hunger, every desolate moment became an invitation to meet myself as I was: open, fragile, and broken. But paper became my outlet, and it became the only way to attract the dark entity slowly back to me. When the tip of my pen touched paper, the closer my Shadow appeared. I wrote it down and drew its shape, catching it by its heel.

I wrangled its calves, its hips, its arms— immortalizing its stature on paper before me. I prevented it from putting on its running shoes and sewed it back onto my sleeve. My journal now a horcrux, and my shadowy friend and I joined again like drops of water.

This process of feeding pain to paper created safe boundaries for my inner darkness to play. It became a ritual of burning secrets to fire. Though music still sang in the background, my Shadow always sung louder—dancing away in cursive ink like the fates and muses. Writing was my fate, and the Shadow was my muse—and whenever I had the urge to run, it welcomed me within the pages and encouraged me to spell my troubles. Its black flames cauterized my tormented heart so I could finally heal.

Although I am healing still, my Shadow is always within me lurking around the pages, begging to be opened again and danced with.

No matter how lonely I feel with darkness, *my old friend*, I am never alone.

NEVADA ♏

I've searched you up which I shouldn't have and though you are difficult to find, I found you indirectly through your betrothed.

I wonder what your apartment looks like, the type of meals being prepared in your kitchen, what color your sheets are, and what your nightly escapades consist of. I imagine you kissing her as if you didn't call me wife before. I wonder how you're fairing as a millennial figuring out adulthood in a town you now call home, approximately 2,636 miles away from where we long stood together. I wonder when you decided to turn your tall and bougee concrete landscape of little dogs and nanny driven strollers in lower Manhattan into a simple, yet desert-like valley filled with old-timers and thrill-seeking tourists in Nevada.

I envision the kind of life I would be living if we were still together and if I'd had a say whether moving to Nevada was what was best at the time; if I'd exchanged a small studio apartment for a large ranch-style house with a backyard and a Dalmatian or maybe German Shepherd who we'd called Brooklyn– not that any of the little details really matter anyways.

What does matter is that in this game of life, you have advanced to the next level where I wish I'd be. Though years have gone by between us now, nothing made me feel as good as the thought that wherever you were, you were doing just fine, average even like me, and trying to triage our dreams into coming true. If we are comparing, which we are, it feels that I've hit quicksand and instead of making it out without distress, I've sunken below into a space that's not my own.

Even though I tell myself "it's okay," that "a setback caused by more schooling and crazy New York City rental prices is okay," none of it changes the fact that I'm still here trapped in the rat maze of the city while you made it out to an open plane with a better view of the stars.

The last time we spoke, you said you were doing better without me, and it kills me to know that this part still holds true.

FLOWER♏

I had asked you if "she came?"

"Yeah," you said, and did not hesitate to answer.

Even after every time I felt disgusted for you going down on me once and never again, for you saying that I tasted different or got fed up trying to make it happen, although we were broken up at the time and you had a *thing* with someone else, nothing made me feel at my lowest up until that point you had said "yeah."

"Yeah, I made her come," as if it was a conquest. A fucking trophy. A long-sought after pleasure that you never got with me. I felt like I have failed both as a woman and a lover because orgasms never came by easily, at least never by you. I felt like she won, and she had something over you that I could never give. Like she was the bigger woman. The one who deserved you. The one you should be with because I wasn't good enough to come too.

It took me a long time to understand that orgasms aren't periods at the end of a sentence. That they do not complete sex nor comment on how satisfactory it had been.

It took me a long time to understand that my body was not solely for you to use or discard after *you* came.

It took me a long time to understand that I was insecure in my own body because of you.

It took another man to open me up like a flower, to spread my legs wide despite my willingness to keep them closed for fear of disappointment, to show me that there was nothing else more powerful than what lay in between. It took this man to show me what love and patience looked like, what care meant in my sexual expression, and for me to come and come plenty of times thereafter.

It took some time to deconstruct the damage you caused and understand that your hesitancy was nothing more than projections for your own failures for not knowing how, or rather not wanting to learn, to please me too. That I am not faulty, but well put together and beautiful in all my everything.

That all this time, the faulty one was you to think it was right to make me feel small the way you did.

BEGINNING
AGAIN

NEW ORLEANS ♌

The last time we came to New Orleans, we fought the whole time. This city reminds you of tension while it reminds me of freedom.

Here we are visiting again, and I'm hoping that this time instead of feeling troubled, this city will feed you the way it has fed me in the past. Something about it is magnetizing, and it calls me back every chance it gets. I am a fool for this city's aura. New Orleans is my place and I hope that in time, she will become yours too.

COLORING OUTSIDE THE LINES ♏

I do believe that there will always be a part of those we loved imprinted in some kind of memory-foam of our existence. A part of their soul lingers on in recollections and what-could-have-been. They play in random thoughts and in dreams decades later, even after they are gone, even after you have forgiven yourself, and even after you are utterly and madly in love with someone else.

Despite moving on, my unconscious still paints a landscape of lost love and betrayal, and in those dreams, I see you reaching for me too. You have that usual smirk on your face and smell like a combination of No. 5 Chewing Gum and Classic Cherry Chapstick. Your Vans slip-ons are all beat up like the time I last encountered them—beige and withered. Staring at your neck, I wonder where my gold rope chain has gone. I wonder whether you had lost it by now or if it now adorns another's collarbones the way I had claimed yours with it in high school.

I wonder what will I remember when I'm older and gray and when memories start to fade?

More than a decade has passed since we touched, and in it I've filled my life with another's lips that are nectarous and sweet like Pepsi in the middle of July and whose skin is like delectable cocoa-butter. Even then, even here when enveloped under his arms and snug into the nook of his neck, my mind gets carried away by a moving cloud that makes me revisit the number of times I counted orange freckles on the bridge of your nose. Was it fifty? Or one-hundred-and-fifty? I cannot remember, but what I do remember was planting a kiss on each one until there were none left to take stock of.

And how could I forget the whispers in the night, the yearning grasp on my naked hips, and the heavy breathing behind my ear? Perhaps by now I've made it all up in what seems to be a fading fever dream.

I know I should remain within my boundaries—the lines I've spent a decade retracing and configuring with my best friend. I know that within them I am happy and cherished. But no matter the days spent between us, I always find myself coloring outside them and creating a whole new world around the confines of the lines.

BAITED ♏

Mother would see me as a rambunctious child who didn't know when to stop.

"You're exactly like your dad," she would say. "Clumsy;" "Don't know when to quit;" "Too much;" and "too into others." Maybe even "lustful" though she never said that word out loud, but I knew she thought it by the way her eyebrow furled whenever I went to the movies with a guy. To her point however, I was quick to fall head over heels in love and since then, I have continued to fall madly at every opportunity.

My legs were always ashy as a child and most days I truly enjoyed my food. I rocked denim shorts, Junk Food t-shirts, and Air Force 1s. Mami dreamt of a little girl that would aspire to be like her and carry out the ambitions she never had the chance to—a girl that acted *like a girl* and would wear dresses and didn't swear. Instead, she was given a child "too" rowdy and "too" like a boy. She held me until I was too much to hold and Papi wasn't within arm's reach to jump to.

As I grew into my teens, I kept mostly to my own. Though I quite preferred it, it was rather lonely. I spent most of my adolescence bouncing between being the outcast, "the weird one," and the most sought after. "She's a slut," the girls in high school whispered as they eyed me talking to their crushes from down the hall. They had no idea that I was just friendly, and my heart was only made for and set on one.

Meanwhile the portrait of my family cracked under the pressure of puberty. They could not deal with the growth of their baby girl and so I searched for another family. I held tightly to the boys who smiled at me. I craved to nestle between the inner vertebrae of a man's back so deeply that I would fuse into their bones as a result. I wanted to be seen and celebrated like the type of recognition and celebration I never had.

"You're not like any girl," I've heard one too many times, yet it still reeled me in like bait. I know I am not like any other girl, and I'm sure every girl who has heard that line feels the same way. This sentiment shone a flashlight on all of us. We were built differently. We were too heavy to hold and so bright that we blinded when shining. We weren't here nor there. We just were, yet we leaped into the arms of anyone who accepted the challenge of bearing such weight. Someone who had extra cups in case we happened to spill over, and who brought sunglasses in preparation for a blown-out fuse.

Whenever those exact words left his mouth, I was

hooked in. His lips smirked and head tilted at the right angle that always caught the sunlight dancing in his eyes. That look made me fall deeper into my shoes. Those deep blue eyes dazzled like the surface of the ocean and had me convinced to dedicate a lifetime to swimming in and make a home there.

He knew what he was doing. This was the bait he used, and with such bait I surrendered. I packed my bags and followed the breadcrumbs. He sang to put me to sleep and made blueberry smoothies to get picky-me to have some fruits. He talked of the old days as if he was from another era and swore to dedicate the future to being different. He drew a home out of dreams and conjured them in the sky. He imagined and talked, and talked more and imagined more, and every time his eyes widened. I listened and began dreaming too. I helped by coloring the insides of the home and dotting each freckle on the children.

He talked a lot of "when we" like "when we move in" this or "when we travel" that, setting intentions for a life bigger than the ones we had at that present moment. I became fixated on holding onto these surreal-like paintings for as long as I could despite the ever-prominent cracks forming at the corners because soon the "when we" became "when you." "When you look different" or "when you tone it down."

He then shifted to a tune I was familiar with. I was "too" loud, "too" angry, "too" caring, "too" loving, "too" selfish. I was just "too" much. Our painting in the sky drastically morphed into a dissection of my body and personality with purple dotted lines circling room for improvement. My dreams then dimmed and signaled a dance more elaborate than I had anticipated at the time. I was in fact "too" into him and completely lost in a whirlpool of his bait.

Though I longed to stay here with him, I did yearn for something "more." Given that I was "too" much, I desired a connection more real, more intimate, and more honest. I longed for a relationship that could provide more than enough. Although in time I broke free from that relationship, my insecurities and overwhelming doubts lingered on for many years thereafter. I had a habit of self-depreciation and often gave in to my distrust.

Instead of his arms that I used to envelop, I now find myself today within ones that are safe. The arms of my best friend have held me steady for the past decade, even though I often pick at them to test whether the seams of our relationship would unravel, as if I didn't trust these arms. *How could they bear all my weight without faltering when I was too much hold for everyone else?* Or perhaps it isn't a test. Maybe, I secretly enjoy the fires I start just to watch something burn.

I've had more than my share of worms on hooks. They left a gaping hole in my cheek, and the road to recovery is slow, but necessary. Looking back, I could see how easy it was to lose my head over some bait. I had been certain that mere morsels were enough to satisfy me, but isn't that what life is all about anyway? *Aren't we supposed to feast on crumbs so we can appreciate a whole banquet when it presented itself?*

Since then, I have no longing to settle for less. I now hold out my hand expecting more from the Universe until I am satiated and my tummy's extended. No longer will I stay content with worms set up as bait. I like to believe my palate has grown far too sophisticated.

I now demand, without compromise, that the whole damn shark is brought to the table instead.

UNSTILL ♌

On Sundays I am reminded of how still the world can be. Outside the cars are slow, and it seems that most people have decided to stay home, too. I look out the window and the world is not as vibrant as it is on a Tuesday morning with folks shuffling and getting into the weekly grind. Nor is it like Friday evenings when bars and restaurants are packed for a celebration of a work week passed. Sundays are not even like Saturdays which are full of adventure, exploration, and a night out in town with good friends. No, Sunday is not like any of those days at all.

Sundays are slow and yearning—yet they whisper promise that tomorrow will come flooding bright lights and loud noise. It is serene as the day calls for rest, but anxious all the same that all good things must come to an end.

Sundays could pour. It could get as messy as we do; we are picked apart by heated words and heated movements inspired by drunken thoughts and drunken actions. A blizzard could grow within us, perhaps an avalanche or two, making us cold.

But Sundays can be slow too, like the way we take our time to meet the morning. I'd wake to find the sun's glow peeking through the blinds as I roll over to you.

With your back turned to me, I wonder when you rolled away in bed, although I already know the answer.

"Because you generate too much heat," you'd say, and I sigh. And we stay in bed for another hour talking about dreams and symbols. When we get the energy to fully wake, we spend the day taking long showers just to sit on the couch. We'd order in our favorite garlicky grandma pizza pie and cuddle in front of the TV watching something old or something new—two cinephiles bonding over Sunday and cheese.

We tend not to say much on Sundays, and an outsider might mistake us for being mad despite how close we are sitting. Normally, they would be right because on any other day, we'd find something to yell about yet continue to love each other even in the rain.

Sundays have taught me to embrace the fluctuation in our temperature. I am not one for stagnant waters and I don't yearn for the calming ripples of a pond. I'm entranced with the dance our waves make downstream and the music the wind sings in the rapids.

But make no mistake that I too desire peace, like the way the sun lightly kisses the skin on a summer day. I fall for the soothing nature that silence brings us when we aren't eager to fill the void with useless words. Without pretense, I am in love with our chaos.

We are water and wildfire, mimicking the blaze and the heat, but we never burn—only smoulder.

RUNAWAY ♌

I don't know why I do it, but I do; and every time I do, I never feel better.

I've been running away for as long as I can remember and to think how I got here; I must look to my mother who also ran away when things got hard. The night she decided to call it quits with my father was a night I'll never forget.

"Please open the door!" My dad pleaded, banging from the outside. I was hiding behind my mother where she ushered me. I so desperately wanted her to open the door to our apartment, but she stood firm in her tracks like a bear protecting her cub. I dared not speak because I felt the floor was already starting to crumble beneath my feet, and my whole world would cease to exist at any moment.

My father's banging grew louder and soon all I could hear was a hard shoving as if he tried to break the door down with his tall and sturdy stature. My mother had enough and went to open the door to let him in, and in mid-thrust, the entryway into the home flew open smacking a mirror behind it. Shards of glass cascaded to the floor as remnants of a broken home.

In disbelief, my mother grabbed my hand and ran. I didn't know where we were going, but little did I know that I would watch her run countless times thereafter. We sought refuge at a friend's place, but never would I have the sanctuary of being with my parents in the same home again.

In her proceeding relationships, I watched my mother grab plates instead of screaming and smash them against the wall. I've watched her purse her lips and hum to hold back tears or whatever hurtful things conjured up in her mind. To this day, I've learned to fear the hum. I've watched her cross the street in the middle of an argument and take the train home by herself. She relied on no one and prided herself on being strong, traits that I've inherited and carried throughout all my relationships too. These are the traits that caused me to not know how to communicate anger or sadness until it was too late.

I've spent too many mornings regretting the actions of the night before and swallowing the pride that's been instilled in me to have in the face of a man. I've learned to apologize and hoped for the best. Despite knowing not to, I still find myself running when scared and when angry and despite how far or how fast I run, I'd still hope that you're not too far along behind, reaching for me to stay.

After years of experiencing my own disappointments and now witnessing my mother slow down to have difficult conversations, I am inclined to slow down too. Through this, I have come to understand my reasons for running are twofold. I'm running away from how I feel when I know words will only get me in to trouble or an intense emotion takes its place in the lack thereof. I'm also running so that I could be stopped because my voice is not loud enough to hold me in place. During chaos, I fear I'd become light like a balloon. I drift and thus forget the home that anchors me.

I've ruined relationships by coming off as selfish and callous, and in the end the calluses in my feet are the least of my worries when you turn your back due to all the running that I do.

Although the urge to run is difficult to resist, I hope now that instead of running away when afraid, I can learn to run back to you instead.

SHARED SOVEREIGNTY ♌

We make love in the shower. It is the sweetest kind of love that I have ever known. In this making, I am undone and made in a single swoop. I melt and become lost in the drops of water trickling down your skin. My body shivers although the heat condenses into sweat over my brows. My eyes widen and I bite my lip as you make your way over me, or rather, through me. And to think that we don't even have sex in the middle of such warm rain. *What becomes of me in such downpour when the only thing raining here is me?*

I am held in your embrace under the shower head. Your arm across my breasts, the other across the threshold of my waist, and your face is hidden in the crook of my neck breathing me in. I wonder, do you smell my day's perfume being washed away—a concoction of the same t-shirt and sweatpants I've worn for the last three days and garlic butter steak from tonight's dinner.

In an act of care, we take turns bathing each other and in an act of service, we do so with pleasure. I watch you as you grab my favorite body wash scented in warm sugar and lavender, and you pour a bit onto a loofah. I am snapped out of a trance when you say, "turn around," and I do so with no hesitation. In what feels like paradise, you scrub my body with such gentleness, stop at the soles of my feet for a massage, and rinse off the suds. I am certain this is your love language. It is your offering to me.

When it is your turn to be washed, I do the same. I rub you in your favorite soap scented with citrus and fir. I stop at your back to knead the trail of knots along your shoulder blades to ease the tension of a warrior's long day. In a pressure as light as a feather, I slowly trace sigils of power, confidence, and devotion along your spine, and I crown you King Leo in this fiery though rainy sovereignty.

After rinsing you off, we hold each other. My arms wrapped around your shoulders, yours around my waist, and to seal the divine work we become lost in a jungle of lips. It is velvety, moist yet silky, slick yet satiny—your lips on mine.

As the edges burn to dark, this vignette of kings and queens, Gods loving Gods, is pure magic.

REMEMBER ♌

I had been the one searching for trouble when I had thought all this time trouble sought me. Trouble took the form of too many glasses of wine—a bit of liquid "courage" to entice me to text another. I had no business talking to another man besides my own after ten at night nor staying up on the phone with him either.

It would always start after three cups in and a thought like *who could I talk to?* I'd text my partner who usually was lost in a video game at this time and was too deep into competition to take a break. Then I'd get an idea like maybe *he's* awake, and then I found myself calling a friend who wasn't really a friend at all, but an audience to my need for attention.

I spent nights talking with this friend about everything. We'd get lost in interpreting dream symbols and psychological thrillers to debating the existence of mankind and religion. He recommended books to read, and we'd exchange excerpts of thought-provoking stories. During the day, we searched through the dollar section at the Strand for the best-yet-tattered old book.

He would carry a small Rhodia notebook and a pencil

with an eraser wherever he went. I hated that he wanted to erase his mistakes when all I wanted was to cross out mine in pen, so the ink stained the lined sheets with echoes of the past. When not in use, his tools remained in his denim button-down pocket for a moment of improvised writing like writers, or over-thinkers, tend to do. He would shake off mainstream everything and romanticize old world philosophers. He swore by the words of the ancient Greeks and dove into their mythological connections to human nature and the divine. We disagreed on almost everything. I'd joke and he'd laugh, and if I ranted, he would listen.

I was moved when he talked of books. He was intellectually stimulating. I was used to being pretty and that was enough for most people of the opposite sex. To engage in a discussion of Kafka's writing style or the effect of Camus's *The Stranger* was a language I'd only dreamt of speaking. It was a change of pace to be heard and seen in this way.

However, it was inevitable that our current would become all muddled up with unintentional signals. He grew to love me, yet I had no love to give back.

But I was in love with who I was with him. I was an accredited poet, an awarded writer, a revered thinker, and animated scholar. I was beauty-and-brains, sarcastic and smart, laid back yet accomplished. An acclaimed version of myself reflected to me throughout our conversations. Parts of myself that were dormant re-birthed into the twinkling stars I had wished upon when I was younger.

"There is no money in writing," my parents said when I told them in seventh grade my aspirations of becoming an author. "You are better off becoming a lawyer or a doctor," they continued, and even today as one of the two, they aren't any prouder. I still haven't outgrown the urge to burrow in my room and write.

Even most of the handsome men I run into were not moved by the waves of poetry like I was. Instead, they were moved by my smile, witty words, and the way they mistook my kindness for flirting. I didn't take myself seriously and that was enough for them not to take me seriously too. I was a pretty face and nothing more.

During my adoration for this accomplished self, I stayed up later to talk to men who cherished my poems all while the man I called home grew to question my intentions. An already quiet man grew quieter, and I'd grown to fear his silence because in it I felt alone. In truth, my current relationship was one of the best things that was born from ruins. Though my partner was no poet, no writer, nor reader, and we never spoke about Kafka except for that one time in English class when we were assigned to read *Metamorphosis*, he took care of me like no other.

Although he didn't know what I was talking about half the time, he loved me raw and encouraged the potential polished stone I was destined to be. Even though we never talked about metaphors or form, I took pleasure in loving him more than I loved anyone, and I'm sure there will be more of him to love throughout my lifetime.

I had not realized that in his acts of service, I drifted asleep and opened to those who knew the right words to say, and in their vision, I became myself reimagined. It was validating, but I felt guilty for allowing myself to swim too far from the shore—far enough for this muse to become that of another's and immortalized in a Rhodia notebook. My friend didn't know it then, but I secretly flipped through that notebook of his and found myself written in graphite. He had animated my mundane and formed my curves in stanzas. Although the feeling was exhilarating, it finally dawned on me then how much I had missed home. His pages were like staring into the mirror of Erised for too long, and despite seeing myself glorified in words, I longed for less illusions.

It was time for me to go back home.

I longed for my favorite gap tooth smile and the familiar arms that held me whenever I was scared. My partner saw me for who I really was: a girl who didn't have it all put together but was on the path of figuring it out. I am messy and, on most days, it would take me hours to write a simple paragraph. I pick up books, but barely get through the ending, and my trajectory is not perfect, but to him that was more than enough. He reminded me to appreciate the process more than the result. He embraced me whenever I felt stuck and reignited the spark through a kiss. He pitched ideas during massages, then ran a bath to help me relax. Although he ruled the jungle, he had no qualms serving me as his queen. With him, I feel perfectly and irrevocably at home.

Home is a reminder to *live* more than to dwell on dreams. All I had to do was remember.

EQUINOX ♏

I am older now and supposedly more mature. Maybe more honest—and if I'm being honest, this time of year invokes in me when I was everything but mature and honest.

I'm sitting on my terrace, out in the open yet safe and confined within my home, with a hard cider in hand and a notebook in the other, basking in the rays of the sun—the same sun who witnessed my cheeks flush red when in sight of him, or him, or any boy— every time an incarnation of my wildest inhibitions being let loose to play.

New York City during this time of year smells different. The smell is reminiscent of sweat and freshly watered grass. The park on the Hudson River is filled with children and their nannies, and the sprinklers are being loosened to bring on the rain. This time of year smells of water surging through the rusted iron pipes of the winter, and a faint aura of salt as the river splashes the piers due to the resurgence of boaters out in the river.

It's the type of weather when it's too cold for a t-shirt, but too hot for a jacket so you opt for a light sweater or a long sleeve, an in-between, and you call your friends to meet you at the pier to indulge in the beginning of a time without restrictions. Spring to summer does that to you. It becomes a city where the adults are inside at work, and the streets are left for the kids to roam.

The dawn of June's heat marks the beginning of first kisses and first losses. A time in which the subway reeks of oily skin and acne—an ode to ripening fruits and pheromone staining pits infused with drugstore fragrances. The transition from spring to summer marks arousal induced sweat and spearmint gum. We wanted to smell good and sprayed what we could afford, even though our secretions overpowered and put the world on notice that we were hungry to be seen.

It was during this time that I would spend hours after school near the water. I would roll in the grass and swing on the swings long enough that I'd come home with a leg full of mosquito bites. I'd sit on the benches secluded behind trees. I would kiss there where no one could see except the sky, the sun, and the stars. These are the very same stars that would later see more of me than I'd like to admit. *My God did the heavens know how much I loved you.* With the sun out, or sunset, or the moon lingering nearby, it did not matter. Summer's love spell was intense. It was tender and sweet, and I'd wish to experience it for years to come.

Every romantic relationship that I have had began

during this transition. Late spring blossomed us like flowers in her garden and pollinated the seeds of underage love, being the truest and purest kind. We were unjaded and unbothered by responsibilities, and free of dense and emotional baggage.

Under this early summer sun, I was brought back to a version of you that I knew long ago—a version that inspired my best summers. Now, as I kick my feet back and finish the rest of this cider while soaking what sunshine is left, I wouldn't have it any other way.

A BLESSING AND A CURSE♏

The first time I encountered death, I threw up.

I was about eight years old enjoying the island of Dominican Republic during summer break. My mother got a call in the middle of the night. Her sister was crying hysterically on the other end. My mother's already tired face quickly turned disheveled. "Oh my god!" She gasped. I didn't know what to make of it. She asked for all the necessary details: the who and the what and the when and the why, and most importantly the how. As the seconds ticked by, I stirred out of sleep and waited anxiously for her to get off the phone.

"What's wrong?" My stepfather asked my mom, but she was too lost in the call to respond.

At that age, I could not fathom what could go wrong. I was still half-asleep and lost in a dream, and most of my day-to-day worries consisted of whether my favorite cartoons would be on TV that night or not.

My mother finally hung up the phone and looked up at me and my stepfather who had been waiting nearby. "Brian is dead!" She exhaled. Brian, my aunt's husband, had died; and without hesitation, I immediately felt a large lump form in my throat.

I didn't know much about death at the time, but what I did know was that it marked the end upon which there was no return. And it was this idea of finality that hit me hard for the first time. It pierced through my stomach and within a few minutes after receiving the devastating news, I had proceeded to vomit all over the floor.

Realizing this type of ending traumatized me. It followed me everywhere I went. I began to see death in everything thereafter. The fallen leaves in the winter, the last day of school, the goodbyes of my father, and the turned backs of lovers. Everywhere I looked, the end was always lingering.

It was this sentiment that left me nauseated in the face of our own ending. It has been a decade since we last spoke, but I still get a visceral reaction whenever I read your old letters serenading our love and claiming to miss nothing more than us together.

A part of me approaches these letters as a woman who isn't afraid of anything. I have lived through the worst of our ending and so much time has passed between us; but as soon as I get through your first words, I am reminded of how wrong I had been. Despite ten long years, your words scare me, or rather scar. Your memory and the way I felt when you turned from being loving to cold still burn like frostbite. My lips quiver and my stomach churns. I am left raw as if it was the first time experiencing our ending, and there is an impending need for me to spill open—my body instinctively rejects you and any pain you caused. Saliva pools at the back of my throat hinting at an involuntary regurgitation. When reading your old love letters, I am left still, quite literally, sick to my stomach.

Reading them now bookmarks an end, and my physiological response is my mourning.

Even though I yearn to rip up the pages, I have come to know that this unease is only a side effect. Maybe it's a curse, but for sure a blessing. Poison in exchange for getting over you still. To confront you today even as a faint whisper of who you once were is the necessary exposure therapy to have me make peace with the finality of our romance. Engaging with your written remnants is that sticky, sweet cherry-flavored yet gut-wrenching medicine that reminds me that I no longer belong here with you.

I belong to the realm of the living, and though we have met our death, I must still go on to new beginnings.

NEW ORLEANS PART II ♌

Like the heat in New Orleans, we are too hot
sometimes; an intensity of passion flows through us
like wildfire. It is the kind where my cheeks flush and
tears flow out the corners of my eyes. A flare so bright
that it licks my insides and rushes the blood to my
chest and to the intimate areas between my legs. A
fire that comes and goes, which is only extinguished
by satisfaction.

When we fight, disagree, and bicker, there is a fire
that grows violently with rage too. One so strong, that
naturally my tears rush down my cheeks to help put it
out. This is the kind of heat that leaves smoldering
scars with memories that can never be snuffed out. A
pyre is made from the both of us and we become
casualties to our own spontaneous combustion.

In us, fire has a home. It moves and swirls in the pit
of our stomachs and at any time, it is capable of being
intensified—for better and for worse. It can fuel
desire or destruction, evoke happiness or melancholy,
and ignite love or hate.

I wish to lean towards the kind of heat that catches
hold of our desires and creates a love where we get
lost in its woods for miles. The kind of wildfire where
its flames are a sense of catharsis to our pain and

soothe our soul; an unstoppable force where tears are not needed to put it out.

This is the kind of fever we wish to be tied to and hope it keeps on increasing from here on out.

CAGED BIRD FREE♏

Have you ever seen the ocean under a starless sky? Its surface is velvet without a speckle of light in sight. It is a moonless black hole and when it is in the pit of your stomach, it is viscous and sweet like molasses. Its density keeps you satiated for a while until it then calls you in. If you were not careful, you could consume yourself from the inside out, become an ouroboros imagined. This is what it is like swallowing hatred to move on from you. Rage would cause one to mistake such poison for nourishment. Little did I know that true nourishment hid in the art of surrender for the waves of fire brought more destruction than it did good.

It had been years since we last spoke, and I for sure thought that I had recovered since then. After swimming through the darkness of my soul, I felt invincible, powerful, and fearless. I made it and I was able to breathe and to be open and to love again. Though I never thought it possible, I came to love myself too. *Did that not count for something?* What I did not know was that the swim to shore was not an act of freedom, but of self-preservation, and deep within I still heard echoes of the girl you drowned gasping for air. She had hidden behind the mask of self-love, bubble baths, and affirmations, but insecurities still managed to creep their way in anyways.

Since our ending, my heart needed a healing that only time and recognition could cure, and though time will have its way whether I liked it or not, the latter was not so easy to come by. It was not until something so small and perhaps silly to most, came into my life that I finally allowed my heart to be released from the cage that our separation and my dismay had constructed.

It is said that the Earth has its healing and provides comfort and compassion through dried dirt and jagged edges. As the home outside of ourselves, the Earth provides nourishment in ways that surpasses our ego. It gives us water. It gives us food. It cultivates and teaches us the lesson of growth, support, and even death. Embedded in its grace, it births radiant stones as an offering for those in need of a little sparkle. It is within these offerings that we find rainbows when we least expect it. Earth granted us magic to make us believe and to center ourselves when we need it most. Whatever the need, this celestial body births crystals to smooth the turbulent waters of our soul. Truth be told I don't believe we deserve such remedial gifts.

I resisted the magic of crystals for so long. I thought, *what pompous creatures we are, taking from the Earth as if Mother was only here to give.* Across history, humans have made a name for themselves in taking. I had understood what destructive creatures we could be given that I was so used to abusing my own flesh; but I have also come to learn that Mother Earth provides what we need when we need it most if we listen and are open to receive its blessings. If we slow down, and if we give, too, in return.

I found my first piece of rhodonite in a small crystal shop in the East Village. While browsing without a piece in mind, it stood out among the others. The crystal shop was beautiful and filled with gems of all shapes and sizes. Many were raw and exquisite. Others were tall and polished. I knew I wanted something that would stay close to my heart, and low and behold something small and shiny caught the corner of my eye—a small rhodonite point held by a golden bail perfect for a matching chain I had at home. I was drawn to it despite not knowing anything about it. Crystals were just pretty to me at that time, and I was oblivious to the old age lessons it had yet to teach me. I purchased the rhodonite and held it in my hands the whole way home.

I did not know that something so small would cause such a huge impact. It whispered songs of forgiveness as only one knows how. Echoes of Billie Holiday's voice would ring loud in my ears singing of a lost lover and a love so profound that it would shake my inner core. It whispered softly and enveloped me in warmth. It held my hand and said, "it is okay to forgive," and in its embrace the grip of a broken heart's chokehold loosened.

I do not want you to mistake this moment as one of weakness nor to believe that all is right between us. It would be a mistake to believe that forgiveness calls for acceptance of wrongdoing. It is in forgiveness that we alleviate our heartaches and make ourselves lighter by detaching ourselves from the burden of pain. Forgiveness asks us to remember the roads that diverged yet met and crashed. To remember that we can rise from the heat of the tar in the road's making rather than melt into it.

I will never forget that you led me to a place I wish never to return to, but I am unsure if I have it in me to continue hating you. Right now, after what feels like an eternity, I am finally tired of thinking of you; and for whatever reason, the Earth extended itself to me in the form of a pink and black rock to let me know that I can let go.

Whether this is the last time I write of you or not, or perhaps your memory fades until I can no longer recall your face, this once-caged bird is at last free to fully love herself again.

IDLE HANDS ♌

When I'm alone, I do things to hurt you
because I miss you.

I look for problems that aren't there
all in the name of missing you.

When you're not here,
my insecurities fester.

The blues convince me to act against us—
Attention being worth the cost.

It is counterintuitive what I do
despite the fact that I love you.

I will admit that I am the creator of mischief.
I start and end with chaos and
bring forth no clear-cut solutions.

To end this cycle, I must wipe the wool
from my eyes so I may express
that I miss you, and that I will love you

without ever crossing you.

PERHAPS FOREVER
THIS TIME

A MOMENT OF GRATITUDE♏

I'd never thought I'd find myself here. It has been easy to bury myself in guilt and self-preservation, and even easier to trick myself into forgiveness, but this doesn't feel quite like that. Instead, this is an offering. A peace meal for being a part of this journey that without you wouldn't have existed. I wouldn't have existed. At least, who I am today—and for that, I thank you.

This is a letter to you and, I'd hope, my last one. I thank you for saying "no" and for saying "I don't think you're the one." I thank you for not giving in when all I wanted was to drown you in my torment. I also thank you for saying the hurtful things you said which allowed me to walk away from whatever we were.

I was a storm all along, and you weren't an exact antidote either. We were chaotic in all weather.

No matter how much we tried, we weren't right and although it had to take me almost ten years to understand, I am confident I may have the guts to finally put you to rest. Put the flames out and let your ashes be that and that alone. I can open the curtains, open the window, air out these sheets to shake you loose from my place. Cleanse this house in herbal smoke and once and for all, push you, gently, on your way.

Even though your winds did drive me into a flurry, I can say even after, even now, I have found peace in this storm.

I WISHED FOR YOU ♌

I cannot remember the exact moment when it all clicked but looking back, I wished for this. I wished for you.

I once held a token gifted to me by a beloved. It was more like a coin and had the words "love token" inscribed with a punched-out heart in the middle. It was given as a reminder that whenever I needed, I could pass it along to redeem his heart.

Standing in his dorm room so many years ago, I held that same token in my hand. I had tears streaming down my face and instead of passing to redeem, I instead made a wish. With my eyes closed tight, I wished for a love so great. I wished for a love where I was valued and where love was equal if not more reciprocated; the type of love that nourishes you in ways one never knew needed nourishment. Above all, I wished to be whole again.

Slowly I opened my eyes and opened my grip, letting the pewter coin fall where it may. Despite my heart being broken, I knew deep within my bones that something greater would come. I had to trust to let go and shed any toxicity that had poisoned me these past few years to be open for what was to come.

I had distrusted your magic at first. In wanting more from a guy who gave less, I unknowingly grew accustomed to chewing with a hole in my mouth where a hook once stood, but then a shift occurred within me that embraced you. During my rebuilding, you were the medicine I needed but did not know and began to feel full once more.

No one has ever touched me like you have. You adore every flaw and kiss them not to pity their imperfection, but to embrace them as they are. You kiss the parts of me that I don't love, the parts everyone else neglected, and they have become your favorite. Your hands rub my sore feet, and your kiss lingers at my belly button. You make me feel beautiful more than anyone else ever has.

For the first time, I saw a run-of-the-mill friendship for what it really was: a connection that gave as much as it received. That moment gifted me the appreciation for my trauma, for without it I would not have been so open in receiving the abundance of your affection and nor would it be so quick to replenish me. Although I made a home out of a wreckage and grew comfortable in its cobwebs, I no longer had to scavenge. Whatever garden grew between you and I became more than enough for us both to feast.

In retrospect, I have given you the best of me for that is all you will ever know. You caught me in a state of despair and yet passed me the pieces as I glued myself back together. Staring at you today, I see how far I have grown to be here. To be able to hold you this long now is a testament to the demons I slayed to get to you, but I'm sure the horrors of my past do not scare you. You are lionhearted after all.

It is funny how only in hindsight can we truly understand what is meant for us. So maybe it was kismet meeting you, and maybe it was destined for me to fall so you could catch me, and not only that but so I could catch you too. From that moment to this day, we continue this dance together supporting each other in a meaningful flow.

You are that token incarnate.

You are my love reawakened.

LOVE POEMS ♌

"It's almost Valentine's Day," you said. "Why don't you start writing some love poems?"

I was taken aback by this statement. I could not remember when I last wrote a love poem, or was inspired to write anything regarding our love, our joy, our happiness. I've fallen into the trap that pain and depression birth the most beautiful work, that inspiration only comes in the guise of tears. I've allowed myself to be in the darkness long enough that I almost forgot what it meant to see light and beauty in all things. And there is light and there is beauty. There are plenty of both that I neglected to cherish within us.

Eleven years have gone by since my undoing and within those eleven years, I've rebuilt myself and my outlook on what it means to be in and have a healthy relationship. For this with you is healthy. It's a relationship without a power structure, although we take turns playing who's on top in the bedroom. We take each other as we are without the nonsense, and without the games.

But I will say, I do miss the games... the teasing and the longing in the game of cat and mouse. The sadistic push-pull that comes with relationships built on insecurity and fragile walls. But this is preferred, let me clear: to be sure that I am loved and that I will be loved. There are no questions about it. Just two truths, no lie. To know that your intentions are not entangled by your own insecurities, my attitude, and other women is exhilarating.

It feels good to be secure, and I don't know how I made it with anything but. It's that

staying in
on the couch
watching movies
eating pizza
drinking wine
not saying a word but
enjoying each other's company
kind of love

and I wouldn't want to experience anything else.

How's that for a love poem?

GENERATIONAL CURSES ♉

There are hard truths I had to learn to take like swallowing a pill dry. They would make their way down my throat despite my yearnings for water. No matter how uncomfortable they made me, I had no choice but to take them in hopes that those truths would be absorbed and, maybe, forgotten. However, even when they made it past my esophagus, they laid in the pit of my stomach and festered like a corrosive battery. Even when one would think they were long gone, those truths still lurked in the shadows causing energy leaks and unsuspecting irritation in every interaction.

Hard truths would linger and gnaw behind the surface waiting to be acknowledged. They would find a way to sneak into every argument, intermingle with the marrows of the spine, and tap dance at the tip of the tongue between every sentence. If I were to get caught up in my own response, I may have missed them for they were subtle, sure, but also loud and deafening all the same. Hard truths became me during my upbringing. Although I have always felt their unease, I did not recognize them until today finally sitting them down and inviting them in for tea.

I now identify them riding on my mother's lips when said she's "putting up with this" for me, sacrificing intimacy and love in exchange for comfort and security.

I see them now in Mama's face when she stayed quiet after Papa blamed her for raising unruly children, and she then spent hours in the kitchen whipping out plates of food to get back in his good graces.

I felt them when La Doña laid her hands upon mine. Her skin was wrinkled with age and sunspots. She tightened her grip and pleaded, "Please become someone," she said. "It is important that you can always rely on yourself."

I heard them in the cries of my stepmother when she reached towards the scissors and destroyed my father's birthday gift thinking that the lavish shirts must have come from his mistresses before his daughter.

I felt them stuck in my throat when the teenage boy I looked up to sat me on his lap at the age of five and reached into my pants, and even now whenever men undress me with their eyes from afar.

I can still feel them whenever a man lifts my arms above my head—my aunt's petrified face flashes before me when her violent boyfriend forcibly pinned her to the bed, and his hand was at her throat commanding utter submission.

In an act of survival, I was taught to not question and bring out the pain of my mother and the women who came before her, but instead to assume the position and stay quiet so that no one would notice how uncomfortable I truly was. I was destined to work for pats on the head and praise for being a good girl; to not react suddenly or else the fire within me would burn.

It is easy to not peel behind the curtain and look deeply into what one saw and pretend that none of it happened, but perhaps playing make believe was what saved the women in my family. Perhaps swallowing these hard truths was an act of self-preservation and healing all along.

This is why I write. It is why writing about what I know leads me down an unprecedented labyrinth and becomes an arduous task to get through. It is why, when words have failed my matriarchal lineage, that I celebrate having finally found our voice even if for now that voice exists through the typing of a keyboard.

Now I wield these fingertips as weapons and type light into the darkness. No more passing along hard truths like curses because cures seemed impossible. I write to break them today. I form incantations to alchemize cries, sarcasm, criticism, and silence, into songs of redemption and freedom. In these words, I seek refuge and grant permission to fight, to love, and to rest. In these words, the faces of my mother, my grandmothers, my aunts, and sisters, and all women who came before me are reflected.

These words are not mine but ours. You no longer need to scream into the abyss for curses were never meant to stay intact. They are meant to break so that blessings can bloom in their cracks.

So be it, and so it is.

THE GREAT HAPPENING ♌

Lately, I've been trapped inside portals. I crack open my journals and I am sucked into the past living moments of what was and what could have been. Other times, my pen takes over and creates a future based on what's to come and what could be.

It seems that I have forgotten to live here in the present with you.

It seems that in between the shouts of what you said and what you haven't, or what you did and what you have not done, I could not see or hear that you are here.

You have always been here.

So quick am I to jump into a fire that has yet to offer real light.

So quick am I to light the match and watch it all burn, and throughout all that longing I have not gotten wind that, despite my tantrums and bullheadedness, you are still here.

You have always been here.

What if the great perhaps I'm searching for is right

here nuzzled between your body rolls? What if it has been resting in the palm of your hand and rubbed into my back as you gently massage the knots? What if it has been riding on the corner of your mouth, a kiss reserved for no one else but me? What if that *great perhaps* became the *great happening*, and it *has* been happening all along?

This is where I ceasefire and put down my arms. I will let you take them, rub your hands on my shoulders as I melt into the crevice of your neck. I would sit with you in silence for the embrace is even more loud and satisfying than anything I could have imagined.

LIKE HOW WE USED TO BE ♌

Last night I dreamt of you. It seemed like a normal dream, but it was anything but ordinary. I had finished a session with our therapist a few hours prior to bed and we spent the time chatting about our goals as couples: five goals that I believed would strengthen our relationship and save us from the path many couples go down—a path towards divorce. Although we are not married, our ten-year relationship has outlasted the national average of seven-year marriages, and at this point a separation is indistinguishably a divorce.

I listed out the goals to accomplish within the year: invest in a home, establish individual boundaries, co-parent a project, explore new methods of intimacy, and take bigger adventures together.

"I am pleased. All the goals you have listed are healthy," our therapist said, and I left the session feeling accomplished. Even if these goals never made it to fruition, establishing them and speaking them to the Universe was half the battle won.

I was in and out of sleep as I usually am in the mornings. Once the clock hits five a.m. my circadian rhythm begins to rouse me out of slumber despite my alarm being set for eight. Those three hours where I am fumbling between states of consciousness are my most imaginative. With every twist and turn my body takes to become comfortable enough to fall back into deep sleep, a new dream begins.

It was during these hours where I found us at a place we have not been in a while. There were a few kids from our high school who took the same subway home after class, and we were among those few. Our mutual friend Jay had introduced us and although you and I weren't exactly friends, we would all ride the train together to the Delancey Street station and transfer different trains towards our respective way home.

In those train rides, you were quiet towards me at first. At the time, many called you shy and during those rides an outsider would say the same, except I have come to learn that your silence was an act of defiance towards me. When you did speak to me, sarcasm exited your mouth.

"I don't get why you're being so mean," I would tell you, believing that I have done nothing to make you turn sour against me. Although you did not verbally respond, your shoulder shrugs were more than enough for me to know that deep inside you were not serious in your hatred. Perhaps you had a persona to keep up, but it was on the verge of unmasking the sweet and sensitive teddy bear I've come to love underneath.

I cannot recall when Jay decided to take another route home, but his decision left us both stranded without him as our leader. Insisting to not waste our time figuring it out, we decided to continue our after-school ritual as if nothing had changed. Soon we would take the train together, almost every day in our senior year.

My dream this morning met us there at the crossroads of the Delancey train station. We had split ways like we normally did, and we waited across platforms for our trains to cross paths—except today I was also waiting for my past Scorpionic lover to meet me. I stood close to the platform edge, turning my head left and right to see if I could catch a glimpse of an incoming train. I could see a small and faint light deep in the middle of the black hole where the train was slithering through in the distance.

I nervously looked around hoping to catch my boyfriend walking towards me right on time. A slight breeze rustled my hair indicating the train was soon approaching the station. The ground beneath me rumbled and I could hear the faint roar of gears turning against the metal tracks. I grew nervous not seeing him in the crowd of people now gathering at the edge too. Any second now the train would make its stop and we would all make our way on it.

I glanced at my phone. There was no message or missed call stating any lateness. "Where are you?" I texted in a hurry. I looked towards the stairs leading above ground hoping I would see his beat-up Vans enter my view, but instead I caught a glimpse of red and white Jordans.

Step by step, a small and thin boy of about one-hundred-and-eighteen pounds came into view. His red shirt was long and below his waist which made him look shorter than he was. We locked eyes then and at the corner of his mouth a small smile appeared: partly devilish, but ninety-nine percent sincere. It was you, my best friend.

"What are you doing here?" I asked in shock as you approached me. I had figured you would be well on your way by now.

"I'm not leaving you alone," you said, and at that moment the train I had been waiting for whooshed behind us making a complete stop. Its gray metallic doors opened, and the crowd stepped inside.

"Come on," you said and grabbed my hand. I held yours tight and followed you into the cool air-conditioned cart where we managed to find a seat by the window. Outside the remaining crowd on the platform began to morph into streaks as the train zipped back into its tunnel. The destination-display flashed and highlighted a route towards our opposite direction without notice.

Though the train progressed on taking us both to unexpected places, we did not seem to mind sitting close and not saying a word. Even in this silence, I felt at ease and had forgotten all about my old flame.

At that moment we were together, not of each other yet but how we used to be, and that was perfectly alright with me.

NEW ORLEANS PART III ♌

This time we made this trip about love.
The love for fun.
The love for food.
The love for us.

Somewhere between
the buttery biscuits and country gravy
from Daisy Dukes,
the crispness of Willie Mae's fried chicken,
the flakiness of Loretta's beignets,
the sweetness of Magnolia's Pralines,
and the Voodoo Daiquiris from Lafitte's,
I found us again the way we were at twenty:

Young,
Inquisitive,
and in Love.

For the past seven years my heart craved to return to
the Crescent City. It was a constant longing that
rendered me asunder and I prayed for every chance
to return.

However, New Orleans had its way with me this time.
I came back home full and tired. My eyes were
bloodshot, and my stomach distended from over-
indulgence. I was swollen and severely in need of a

detox. But I now believe, even though it pains me to say, that I may have had my fill of this city. That in truth, what I was craving all this time was not the southern heat nor the live jazz, but us. Despite the two-week hangover upon our return home to New York, NOLA did not fail in casting its magic on us.

This time instead of searching for the Big Easy, the Big Easy found us.

It found us as teenagers again taking shots on Bourbon Street.

It found us on our first date within our quest for treats in the French Market.

It found us as fearless explorers taking unexpected turns in Tremé.

It found us laughing and dancing and making love every night as if we haven't been fighting.
As if 2022 did not attempt to break us open.

Yeah, this city reunited us.

I may have longed for New Orleans,
but I am certainly now content just being
here in *our* city with you.

AN ALTAR OF MY OWN ♉

I cannot forget to put on lotion when you are not here. I have grown accustomed to holding off for I know that you would be patiently waiting until I came out of the shower and was completely dried to lather me up. Though I appreciate you taking care of me, the way you massage petroleum jelly on the calluses of my feet, I must remember that I can take care of myself too. That I *must* take care of myself.

If I was not careful, I would leave my hair in a knotted mess, my elbows and knees would become white and ashy, and my lips chapped. It is easier to wait for you and give you this moment of awe than it is for me to bring consciousness to the folds of my skin, the marks that stretch across my bottom, the scars on my legs, and the dimples in my thighs. It is easy to turn away from my small breasts, the dips of my hips, and the ripples my stomach makes when I sit down.

For you this opportunity is a means of reverence. For me it is a reminder of disappointments. It is a reminder that I had left my prime even though I did not appreciate my body any more back then. Though I am unsettled with the tasks that lay before me, I know it must be done.

I reach for the lavender scented lotion and with a dollop of it I rub my hands together. Starting at my ankles, I make my way upwards. My hands go in circular motion smearing cream over my dry skin. I focus heavily on my knees where many old wounds have long healed and certain spots have become discolored. I remind myself of all the times I fell off my bike when I was a kid. Although I wish the scars farewell, I thank them for a childhood that overall had been good to me.

I massage more lotion into my inner thighs over the cellulite that has accumulated over the years. Fighting the urge to shake my head, my thumbs knead acceptance in the forms of hearts.

I swallow my mother's disapproval as I rub the lotion over my backside. Her tongue clicking as my bottom swelled, the curves of my body looking more distinctly my own and less of hers. I was no longer twinning at one-hundred-and-fifteen-pounds and instead have grown an asset highly sought after. Lost between the curves, I cannot recall the last time she called me beautiful instead.

I focus on my stomach and the pouch that made its way there, taking deep breaths. This stomach indulges when life is good and starves when it was not. I am in a constant battle between flat and bloat, and no matter how many sit-ups or crunches I do, my love for carbs will not allow a difference. My hands rest over my belly button and the tip of my thumbs and pointer finger touch forming an upside-down triangle. Soon this stomach will give way to a child and for that possibility, I am grateful for what is to come.

I cup my breasts and swallow back tears. I spent most of my adolescence hating them. I pushed them together with all sorts of tape and uncomfortable bras and pulled down my V-necks as low as I could to show the world what little cleavage they made. While all the girl's breasts grew in middle school, mine stayed the same. The boys made jokes and the big breasted girls roped me into what they called the "itty-bitty-titty-committee."

I had searched within the woman in my family looking for someone to blame, but in the end, I cursed myself and vowed to get a breast augmentation the first chance I got. Instead, I got a boyfriend who was fixated on fixing me and soon delivered an ultimatum on a silver platter: "I can't be with you unless you change them," he said. And after years of trying to make it work, I walked away despite my insides drowning. Little did I know that I would spend the next two years recovering from this massive heartbreak and another eight reconfiguring what love truly is.

I now push my breasts together and feel their weight on my palms. They are warm and comforting like two small dinner rolls with butter, and although they were not enough then, I do believe they are quite enough now.

I finish off with petroleum jelly on my feet and take my time in the middle of my soles. My feet have carried me thus far for the past twenty-nine years. They have slowed down in moments of embrace and sped up when my inner urge to run kicked in. I spend more time on the right foot specifically, gently lining with my finger where I had broken the bone four months prior. It was a fracture that forced me to slow down and not get ahead of myself—a lesson that I have been trying to learn for a decade and I am sure will take me a lifetime to fully comprehend.

To finish, I rubbed the remaining lotion up and down my arms. Though I prefer this ritual of sorts when you do it, maybe it is time I reclaimed this altar, or perhaps we share it so we can both love this body together.

AN ADULT THOUGH CHILD♏

"Grow up, little girl," were your last words to me.

Your text message encased in a blue bubble seared my eyes. My stomach dropped to the floor without hesitation, and my phone followed right after falling out of my hands. In a fit of dismay, I too dropped and, in an instant, tears gushed from my eyes. Your words rang louder in my head. Grow up? Little girl? GROW UP! LITTLE GIRL! GROW! UP! LITTLE! GIRL!

I curled into a fetal position naturally emulating your sentiments. Though not intended, I reverted to the callow girl who fell for you when we were younger, though I am also cowering during this weaning off period that is our breakup. Despite knowing we were young, I felt forever with you. Was that not enough commitment to grant me maturity?

Throughout the time and space when we met at twelve, then coupled at seventeen and again at twenty, I can now say I have done more growing than I have ever intended to in what feels like a short period of life. Each of our reunions brought baggage and made us pack-on a few years thereafter. The effects of our collision can still be felt. We are the ripples from our own earthquakes.

I recall the summer of 2005 when I wished with all my might to age sooner. Your sandy blonde hair reminded me of California and all I knew of California, here in the East Coast amid aggressive winters and rap bars, were sounds of The Beach Boys. Every thought of you came accompanied by their notions of growing older and running away with your sweetheart to coastal lands. Every time they played on the radio, I felt outed by the Universe and found ways to shrink myself so that no one would notice I was mourning my summer crush.

My mother had witnessed our first kiss and since then made me vow to never see you again. To make her happy, I pushed you away and kept myself hidden inside throughout the break. My appetite decreased and I felt an immense longing deep within my stomach to age into an adult when freedom would be easy to come by. *Perhaps when I'm older, we could be together at last*, I thought. Unbeknownst to me, I had spoken a prophecy into existence and that we would continue to cross paths despite my mother's wishes.

Almost thirty years old now and life is moving too fast. I crave for it to slow down. I desperately want to seize fleeting moments in a jar for safe keeping but become devastated to find that no matter my efforts, nothing gold can stay. *But isn't it true that life is all about the gold no matter how long it sparkles?* I am growing still and have come to find that I am no less a child even as an adult. If to grow up means to be complacent, to accept a life that is nothing more than chasing down fireflies, then I do not want any part of it. I don't want to chase fireflies and lock them in a 3" x 5" mason jar. No, I want to run with them, dance into the night, and fall asleep within the tall grass under the stars. I don't long to forget and to sit still. I long to feel, and cackle, and howl loudly. I long to live despite the ticking of time, and to be immersed in all colors of the moon.

If loving you and showing it was childish, I don't look forward to being an adult. I refuse to be imprisoned by fear, to be swept up by disappointment that I become frigid, dispassionate, and worst of all petrified to jump when Faith meets me at the precipice.

I refuse to grow up even if it makes me a fool. Staying soft and choosing love is and always will be worth the leap.

REQUIEM ♏

I am no stranger to the waves of grief.

Anger came first as denial was never my strong suit. I reverted to writing curses and listed all your cons: choosing friends over me whenever I felt down or refusing to answer my calls when we fought. Oftentimes, you kept me on a string like a yo-yo and I whirled up and down between admiring you and despising you. You'd furrow your brows, pout your lips, and let your ocean eyes ask for pardon strapping me back within your hand in mere seconds. Yet just as quickly as you pulled me in, your watery gaze would freeze, flinging me over the edge once more.

Bargaining came next. I wrote letters in your name and ended them with "please give me another chance." I appealed to you as if I was on trial and like God, you held my fate. Judgment came in your silence.

I stayed in depression. I sketched your Cupid's bow in failed attempts to say goodbye. I wrote the absolute best of you, recording the reasons why I fell hard not once but thrice, then proceeded to cry into my pillow into the dead of night. I was a banshee wailing old love songs in the shower and my tears poured harder than the water from the spout that washed over me.

Maybe the process of spilling ink onto paper during all stages was the main point after all. Swaying between messy emotions was necessary to come to know what we were missing all along: traits like loyalty, truthfulness, and kindness.

Conceivably, writing was also a means of mourning your loss. The day we fell apart was also the day you died yet penning my thoughts of you became the only way to hold onto your Ghost despite the fear it also caused. I've become far too familiar with having Ghosts around, lugging them like baggage in every conversation and encounter, that I trembled at the onset of loneliness if they all departed too. Abuse, neglect, betrayal, and tragedy, I took some pride that despite my unease, these Ghosts defined me; yours joined the rest and like the others, haunted me with pride.

Perhaps some would call this stage acceptance, but I refuse to come to terms with how this story could have ended if I'd allowed these Ghosts to stay with me forever. I've come to believe there is a sixth stage that no one talks about.

I've learned that silence brought more peace than the Ghosts who wailed around me. With all the courage I could muster, I fed these Ghosts crumbs. Each time I offered less of myself until they starved and ceased to come back. I made my body uninhabitable for Ghosts like yours fed on anguish. Instead of harboring the suffering they liked, I filled myself with whatever bit of joy I could find. I chose the warmth of the sun instead of mourning the summer we grew out of. I made new memories by the pier with new friends instead of safeguarding signposts of ours. I gave into the sweetness of others instead of remaining cynical of strangers. *Surely, there are good people out there too,* I believed. I talked things out instead of holding them in.

I hugged myself when I needed and laughed out loud when I found something funny. I like to think that I laughed so loudly that I instead scared them. My cackling, like that of an old hag during the sabbath, had finally chased the Ghosts, even yours, away. Years passed on and your Ghost seldomly appeared in dreams but left as quickly as it came. Choosing to fill my heart with the little things became the exorcism that I never intended but had always needed. This part is called reclamation.

I write these words now in reflection of mine as I flip through my old and tattered journals, let this be the wave in which I rise. Let this be the part where I make it to shore and leave behind a tidal of destruction. Let this become the part where I close our chapter for good and sever the cord between you and me. Let this be the funeral I resisted attending, and with honor and with grace, may I finally lay your Ghost down too to rest.

AN *AFTER*WORD ON WORDS ☿

Words almost broke me, but words also saved my life.

When life was meaningless and I lacked the energy to get out of bed, I still mustered the energy to write. I wrote what I was feeling. I wrote what I dreamed. I wrote as if I would forget and trust me all I wanted to do was forget; but, funny thing too—I also wanted to remember. I wanted to remember for moments like today when I'm feeling nostalgic and am rereading what looks to be the evolution of a broken heart. I've come to discover that words were what saved me.

Words saved me from myself when I desired to crawl to the edge of the abyss and jump.

I wanted the void to take me.
I wanted the night to make love to me.
I wanted to succumb to death's taste.

So, I wrote love letters to the night and begged for it to fuck me to oblivion, but time and time again it refused because I had more words to give.

More stories to write.
More life to express.

It seems that I had enough sparkle in my eyes for the darkness and they kept spitting me back out to face my own sadness.

"Write it out" they said, and I did. I wrote everything. Words on words on words. Some words were ugly, and some words scarred but they provided meaning to broken parts. They mended me back together again with gold. I took whatever mess existed in my thoughts and I painted them in the sky to make sense of their chaos.

With its vast embrace, the Cosmos lifted me from the shadows and held me close to the sun whose warmth I have long forgotten. It consumed me thus giving birth to me once more. Within the corners of my mind where there seemed to be no way out, words opened the door to the possibility. They were unable to make me anew, but they instead gave me something more: a torch to guide through the black.

The words written, my words now, continue to exude a star into being—every word forever lighting the night.

ACKNOWLEDGMENTS

I knew when writing in my journal as a distraught teen that it would one day lead to a book. I had thought that it would inevitably be a book about heartbreak. Then compiling the pieces and creating new ones for the making of this one, I am led to believe that it has become about something more.

This book is about writing and its ability to save us when we need it the most. There is something so cathartic about revisiting our traumas in words where we get to take our time, mourn again, and take back the narrative. I was empowered in telling my story.

However, it is also true that this book is not about heartbreak or writing at all. It is about love—love found in the darkest of places, love found within the self, and love found when the opportunity takes you by force, if you surrender to it. I could have easily shied away from love when it came knocking on my door. I could have easily turned away given how dirty it often played with me before, but for no reason other than I am human, I did not. I carry my heart on my sleeve as a memento to love more, to love harder, and to love deeper. I recommend, dear reader, that you do the same.

I want to thank my partner Loek for being by my side

during the dark depths of my soul these past ten years. I don't know how you did it. Although I did not always listen, you were a voice of reason and comfort when I needed it most. I know this book was not the easiest for you to read and for that I appreciate all your support despite of, and words of encouragement when I thought publishing a book was a pipe dream. I sincerely am grateful for the time and dedication you spent reading through rough drafts and putting up with me as I disrupted your own work with out loud readings of my own. This book would not have been made possible if it weren't for you. I love you, Koko.

I want to also thank my therapist TJ who without your guidance late last year, I may have dangerously acted over and against love for the third time.

March 2023

ABOUT THE AUTHOR ♉

C. M. ESCABI is a writer immersed in poetry and prose who blends the art of magic and spell crafting into her words. She is the head witch in charge of Ultramagica® by where one could find tarot readings, candles, spell kits, and crystals for an intentional spiritual practice. Escabi is also the host of *Coming*

Out of the Broom Closet, a live series where she interviews creators and magic makers who redefine healing and are leaders in their own craft. She hosts writing workshops and facilitates the writing group *Spell Work Poetry Circle*. She and her poetry have been featured in *Vice News*.

She lives in New York City and spends her time crafting candles, binging on pizza, and dreaming of far-flung places, all while snuggling with her two familiars, Max and Gigi. She can be found slinging cards for the collective on a Friday or getting lost in the rainbows of a quartz crystal during a sale. She is a Taurus Sun, Cancer Moon, and Leo Rising.

This is a Spill, This is a Spell is her first book.

To learn more and get in contact, please send an email to **ultramagica.info@gmail.com**

Visit her online shop for more writing, to book a tarot session, and purchase ritual tools at **www.ultramagica.com**.

She can also be found @ultramagica on Instagram, Tik Tok, Threads, Twitter, and YouTube.

Made in the USA
Middletown, DE
14 October 2023